GW00459826

TRIM FOR LIFE

Dr Garry Egger MPH PhD

ALLEN & UNWIN

With appreciation to Matthew O'Neil BSpSci, DipNut for his contributions to the manuscript.

Copyright © Garry Egger, 1997
Cartoons by Sue Plater

All rights reserved. No part of this book may be reproduced or transmitted in any form or by any means, electronic or mechanical, including photocopying, recording or by any information storage and retrieval system, without prior permission in writing from the publisher.

First published in 1997 by
Allen & Unwin
9 Atchison Street, St Leonards NSW 2065 Australia
Phone: (61 2) 9901 4088
Fax: (61 2) 9906 2218
E-mail: frontdesk@allen-unwin.com.au
URL: http://www.allen-unwin.com.au

National Library of Australia
Cataloguing-in-Publication entry:

Egger, Garry.
    Trim for life: 201 tips for effective weight control.

    Bibliography.
    Includes index.
    ISBN 1 86448 466 7.

    1. Weight loss. I. Title.

613.7

Set in 10/12.5 pt Caslon 224 by DOCUPRO, Sydney
Printed and bound by Southwood Press, Sydney

10 9 8 7 6 5 4 3 2 1

CONTENTS

INTRODUCTION

Science and weight control

The field of weight control is dotted with landmines, all posing as 'friendly passage'. At every turn there's someone trying to sell you something, usually disguised in technical jargon and offering 'amazing', 'fantastic', or 'unbelievable' results from some product or program with a previously undiscovered 'magic' or 'secret' ingredient.

Little wonder the average punter is confused!

Like all health fads, weight control promises follow the course of least resistance. Everybody wants to be trim. Moreover, they want it overnight. But the gradual rise of obesity in modern Western societies means that the opposite is slowly happening: the average gain in body weight in the Western world, over the past 15 years for example, has been at the rate of 1 g per day or roughly 1 kg every three years. By now 55% of men and 35% of women in Australia and New Zealand, and even more in North America, are regarded as overweight or obese, and these percentages are increasing at around 1% per year.

Weight control scams have always been prolific. But under these conditions they're almost as prevalent as the problem with which they're purporting to deal. The mere fact that the population keeps on getting fatter suggests that nothing that has been tried to date works—at least not on a large scale. This in turn suggests that we've been looking at the problem in the wrong way. Maybe, just maybe, the first thing that springs to mind at the mention of the term 'weight loss', i.e. dieting, is the wrong way of dealing with the problem. More to the point, it could be part of the problem. Similarly, maybe none of our ideas about exercise for fitness and sports performance are related to the type of exercise needed for fat loss. And if this is the case, maybe we've been barking up the wrong tree. Does the whole tree need a good shake, if for no other reason than to help shake out the rotten apples?

To some extent this is already happening. Scientific research in the field of obesity and body fatness has increased enormously in recent times. So much so that it would not be untrue to say that there has been more published scientifically on the topic in the last two decades than in the whole of human history before that. As a result we're learning heaps. But much of this information lies locked up in universities and research establishments while quick-buck marketers have a field day with pseudo-science.

Changing the model for weight loss

What is clear is that the old model of body weight which was based simply on energy in (food) minus energy out (exercise), is wrong. This is a 'physics' type model which implies no flexibility in the system, no reaction of the human body to change (such as a change in appetite with an increase in exercise).

Using this model it's been calculated that if a man ate an extra slice of toast and marmalade each day for 40 years of his life, he'd put on around 187 kg. As only very few people ever get to this weight, the proposition is clearly absurd. The model doesn't work. And notions such as calorie counting and dieting which have come from this way of thinking are equally outdated. It might be comforting for you to know this at the outset: that the vast majority of popular magazine 'diet of the week' programs are not only useless, they can be positively counter-productive! Dieting is dead. And if it isn't, then as far as weight control is concerned it should be.

A new model for weight management therefore is needed. This has to take into account the total environment as well as the genetic and behavioural aspects of the individual. We know now that genes are important, but we also know that the genetic predisposition to obesity is unlikely to be fully realised in an inhospitable environment (one where food is not allowed to take control).

A new model also has to consider the adjustments that the body makes any time there's a change in energy balance which, over the long term, often serve to prevent any long-term losses of weight. These are adjustments like increases in appetite with increased exercise, or decreases in metabolic rate with decreased food intake. Changes like this are designed to maintain the status quo in the face of changing conditions—an obviously desirable characteristic in times of scarcity, but not so useful in times of excess.

Finally, a new approach has to consider the recent nutritional and exercise research which shows that it's the *type*, more so than the *amount*, of food eaten which is important and the *duration*, rather than the *intensity*, of exercise carried out which have the greatest overall impact on energy balance.

A model incorporating all of these components is shown in the diagram below. These have been developed and discussed in detail in one of my more technical publications (Egger and Swinburn, *The Fat Loss Leaders Handbook*,

AN ECOLOGICAL PARADIGM FOR
WEIGHT CONTROL

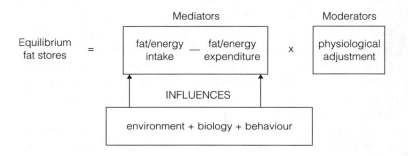

Sydney, Allen & Unwin, 1996) and published in the *British Journal of Medicine* (1996).

This book draws on a collection of accepted scientific principles within each of the components of the model. Each chapter represents a different component of the model. The book is not meant to form a weight control program as such, and in a sense this may not be necessary anyway.

The main program from which the information has sprung is 'GutBusters', the first major men's 'waist control' program developed in Australia, initially in conjunction with the NSW Health Department. The GutBuster program is blessed with a top-level scientific advisory board which guarantees it's accuracy, ensuring that no fads, gimmicks or faulty premises can infiltrate the rigour of the content material.

Each tip listed herein has, in the main, a scientific reference for those wishing to check its academic validity. References are listed in order in the back of the book. Where no reference is included, the suggestion is based on my own empirical experience and a logical physiological explanation (which, I agree, may need to be verified at some later time). I've used the principles of 'do no harm' and 'don't let it cost' in the meantime. I've also avoided the faddists' practice of preaching 'amazing' results from any of these suggestions. All need to be considered carefully within the context of a healthy lifestyle, with no special emphasis given to any particular tip.

Weight loss and change

To lose weight, by definition, requires change. And there are really only two types of change which are effective. These are: *eating differently* and *moving more*. You'll notice that this doesn't imply *eating less*, or *exercising more*, in the traditional sense of the words. Within these two approaches there are numerous recommendations which can help to effect an ultimate change in energy balance, the contrast between the amount of energy taken in (food) and the amount of energy used up (exercise). This book presents a selection of these recommendations which have some scientific support.

Each tip is meant to stand on its own. So if you want to pick up the book at meal-time, between kids' baths or even while seated in the smallest room in the house, you can start at any point. For this reason, some of the tips may appear slightly repetitious, although I've tried to avoid this as much as possible.

The basic ideas for the book came from the *Waist Watch* Newsletter, a summary of the latest scientific findings in weight control and metabolism, which I have edited since 1993. All of these findings have been put into practical terms so they can be put straight into action. And while no one recommendation is likely to see you change your body shape overnight, regular use of many of the ideas could have a long-term effect on your body weight and, even if nothing else, are likely to improve your overall health.

1
NUTRITION

You'd be excused for thinking that food is food, and that once you know about what makes you fat, that's all you need to know. But it's not quite as easy as that. New research shows different ways in which food works. Foods once thought to be fattening are now often considered essential ingredients in the fat management recipe. The starchy carbohydrates—potatoes, pasta and rice—*aren't* fattening. If anything, they fill you up and prevent you from going after the 'greasies'. The burden of restrictive diets and the hunger inevitably accompanying them is therefore no longer a prerequisite for success in weight management. Discovering that results can be achieved by eating differently, not less, may be a welcome surprise—but then, this book is about surprises!

1.   Don't fast

Contrary to popular opinion, fasting doesn't cleanse the system or eliminate fat-producing toxins. Unfortunately, fasting eliminates vital minerals and other elements, not toxins.

During World War II, Dr Ancel Keys conducted a series of fasting experiments on a group of conscientious objectors (research that wouldn't be allowed today). The men were put on a semi-starvation diet (1570 kcal/6560 kJ) which provided less than half the normal amount eaten, and were required to lose 19–28% of body weight. If a man wasn't on target to lose this, his food was cut further. Vigorous exercise was also part of the regimen. As the study progressed, the men experienced the following:

Physical
- A decrease in work output heart rate by 50%
- Decreased body temperature, the feeling of being cold all the time
- Weakness and tiredness
- Giddiness and fainting on rising
- Muscle cramps, eye aches, ulcers, sores and loss of hair
- A fall in basal metabolic rate of almost 40%

Psychological
- Apathy, irritability, moodiness and depression
- Impaired judgment and decreased libido
- An increase in psychosis and violence

(Does this read like your last diet?)

They also became preoccupied with thinking about food (who could blame them!) and cravings increased. To deal with this, some men actually took up smoking. After they were returned to their normal food intake, some continued to have psychological disturbances and, to make up for the period of deprivation, compensated by eating up to 200% of what they normally ate before the study began. As a result, they gained fat rapidly, making them fatter than they were before the ordeal.

From this you can see why starvation, or even short-term fasting, isn't the answer. Fasting doesn't reduce weight over the long term. It may even increase it!

2.   Don't diet

The word 'diet' has become synonymous with a structured reduction in food intake. Most diets involve either a strict regime of daily food intake, or a rigid control over types and quantities of food eaten or restricted.

There are a number of reasons why this doesn't work in weight loss:

1. Going on a diet means coming off it at some stage, meaning that all that's lost will eventually be regained (probably with interest). Permanent weight loss requires permanent changes. Basically, in weight control, if it's not something that can be done for a lifetime, it won't work.

2. Food (energy) restriction (particularly with no increase in exercise) leads to a reduction in the body's metabolic rate which can be even greater than the loss of body mass. For example, a 10% loss in body mass from dieting can lead to a 20% reduction in metabolic rate. As metabolic rate makes up about 70% of our total daily energy use, any reduction can lead to an increased ability to conserve energy (or store fat). Even under continued dieting, this would mean at least a levelling out, or plateauing, of fat loss. But as most people can't maintain a diet, and therefore go back to eating more, the reduced rate of energy would inevitably lead to an *increase* in body weight.

3. Much of the weight lost during a diet (again without exercise) is lean body mass (mainly muscle). This can be as much as 25% in an average sized person. (In a lean person it can be even higher because they have less fat to lose.) However, muscle is a prime source of energy use and hence muscle loss will reduce metabolism. When weight is regained after eating again, less of the regained weight will be muscle. The consequence then of a short-term diet is *increased* weight, but in the form

of more fat than may otherwise occur with gradual weight gain.

It's true that 'dieting can make you fat'. Avoid diets like you'd avoid the plague.

4. Diets are too hard. Where food is tempting and abundant—as it is today—'dieting' symbolises masochism. If hunger increases, there's a far greater chance you'll give in and bingeing will result.
5. Diets are the first casualty of stress. People who are 'restrained' eaters are those most likely to drop their bundle when faced with stress, grief or depression—as we all are from time to time. Because food is often a source of comfort, stress can then be a signal to over-eat, in which case you can wind up worse off than you were before.
6. Diets are often not nutritionally balanced. Each commercial diet plan has its gimmick. Many of these, such as low-carbohydrate, low-fat, 'fruit juice' or other special 'wonder food' diets, can lead to deficiencies of some of the major nutrients required by the body. Some well known diets (e.g. the Atkins diet) have even been legally challenged because of these potential risks.

For all of these reasons it's true that 'dieting can make you fat'. Avoid diets like you'd avoid the plague!

3.   Don't eat less than 1200 kcal a day—unless under strict medical supervision

Resting metabolic rate (RMR), or the rate at which the body burns energy at rest, can be estimated by formulae based on sex and weight and age. Use the following table to find your RMR in kilojoules/day; divide by 4.2 to give you a result in kilocalories.

Males	10–18 years	$(74 \times \text{weight kg}) + 2754$
	18–30	$(63 \times \text{weight kg}) + 2896$
	30–60	$(48 \times \text{weight kg}) + 3653$
	over 60	$(49 \times \text{weight kg}) + 2459$
Females	10–18 years	$(56 \times \text{weight kg}) + 2898$
	18–30	$(62 \times \text{weight kg}) + 2036$
	30–60	$(34 \times \text{weight kg}) + 3538$
	over 60	$(38 \times \text{weight kg}) + 2755$

Using this table it can be seen that even a 25 year old, 50 kg female would have an RMR of 1222 kilocalories. This means that around 1222 kcals of food is required to maintain energy balance (i.e. no gain or loss of weight) in this person at rest. Depending on the activity level involved, the energy requirement can vary by a multiple of up to 2.4 times the RMR. So a relatively active 50 kg woman might require a daily food intake of RMR × 2.0 = 2444 kcals—just to maintain weight!

Less than this will cause a loss in body weight. But too much less can cause the body to adjust radically to the change through those mechanisms discussed in Tip 2 above. This means that over the long term, fat gain rather than fat loss may be the ultimate outcome. A daily input of around 1200–1400 kcals could be regarded as the lowest level for safe, effective, long-term fat loss for most people.

4. Avoid cafeteria-style foods

The 'cafeteria diet' is a term used to describe snacks—foods that are high in fats and sugars—characteristic of modern Western cultures. Research with Puma Native Americans in the United States, allowing them free access to vending machines offering a variety of familiar palatable foods, has shown that this can increase energy intake by over 50%. Around 40% of the extra intake is in the form of fat, and 48% in carbohydrate.

Measures of the rate at which nutrients are oxidised—or burned up—as energy, showed that extra carbohydrate intake results in extra carbohydrate being oxidised. However, extra fat intake had no such effect, meaning this fat would be stored as extra body fat. The cafeteria diet not only results in more being eaten, but in more fat being stored. Beware the cafeteria diet.

5. Develop your own lifestyle eating plan that's low in fat

Fat in food is high in energy (9 kcals/g versus 4 kcals/g for carbohydrate or protein). Fat is also stored in the body with greater efficiency. Finally, fat tends to increase rather than decrease the appetite and the amount of total food which can be eaten at a sitting. So reducing fat in the diet is now accepted as being perhaps the single most effective control against obesity. But whether this can be done without a strictly laid out low-fat diet plan is open to question.

In contrast to *ad libitum* (i.e. 'free choice') eating, diet plans where people are advised which foods they should eat in minimal amounts have usually been the order of the day. But research from the Agricultural University in Denmark suggests this should no longer be so.

Scientists were investigating a food program where a group of men and women were told where fats were in foods and then asked to keep these foods to a minimum. Those on this program were compared with a group of controls on a normal diet after 11 weeks; it was found that they actually lost more weight—even though they ate no less in total calories!

Weight loss was also quite clearly from fat stores, rather than muscle stores, suggesting a greater long-term maintenance of fat loss, because this is less likely to reduce metabolic rates. Those with the highest levels of fat at the beginning of the program also had the greatest fat losses—again a change in the right direction.

In assessing their results, the Danish researchers point out the inadequacies of weight-reducing diets. They suggest that with a reduction in fat in the diet, people can avoid obsessive calorie counting, but still lose weight—and in a healthy manner.

6.   Eat a wide variety of foods

If you eat from only a small variety of fatty foods every day, it's easy to get fat. This was observed in a comparison of eating habits between lean and obese people in Nevada. The obese people ate less food types than the lean and these foods were generally higher in fat. In a previous study, low scores on an index of food variety were found to be associated with almost all the established cardiovascular risk factors.

A long-term over-intake of fat is the best way to keep or increase fat on the body. To combat this, even without focusing directly on dietary fat, just increasing the selection of foods is a wise move. The first paragraph of most Government dietary guidelines usually states that we should '. . . enjoy a wide variety of nutritious foods'. These include breads, cereals (breakfast cereals, pasta, rice), vegetables, legumes, meats, chicken, fish, eggs, nuts, milk, cheese and yoghurt.

7.   Graze, don't gorge

If you eat the same type and amount of food in a day, does it really matter how or when you actually eat it? It appears that it does. A grazing pattern with smaller meals eaten more often may in fact be better than a gorging pattern where there are only 1–2 large meals and little else each day.

> **Eating more frequently may
> help minimise hunger levels
> during the day and
> therefore help you to eat
> less total energy.**

Researchers at Laval University in Canada compared the effect on metabolism of food consumed in one large meal (653 kcal) versus four small meals (163 kcal each) at 40 minute intervals. There was a larger overall increase in metabolic rate after eating with the four smaller meals than with one large meal. Fat utilisation for body fuel was also greater with the four meal pattern.

Eating more often can also help minimise hunger levels during the day and therefore help you to eat less overall. If you've just had breakfast and you plan to eat nothing until dinner time, you may not get there before the 'bear in your belly' gets the better of you. For these reasons it's better to graze rather than gorge.

8.   Eat for health as well as weight control

The motivation for many people to eat better is to lose weight. But efforts to do this, for example by cutting back on fat, aren't entirely without hazard, as was revealed in a study of the dietary habits of over 3000 Australians in 1990. Researchers separated the group into high and low fat consumers. Those on the lower fat intakes achieved this by restricting meats and dairy products, which resulted in a reduced intake of vitamins A and B12 and the mineral zinc.

This is not surprising considering the poor reputation

that meats and dairy foods have with slimmers. Often seen as fatty, they're unnecessarily cut back or eliminated from the diet. This is a dangerous trend which has sparked health campaigns to inform consumers about the benefits of leaner varieties of meats (e.g. lean beef and trim lamb) and lower fat milks and cheeses.

The authors of the Australian research concluded that 'for optimal effect, nutrition messages about specific nutrients should not be given in isolation but in the context of a general "healthy eating" message'. This makes perfect sense. If you've developed a fat phobia, regain a healthy perspective.

9. Exclude, modify, substitute or replace—it's your choice!

There's an infinite combination of foods which can make up an eating plan for successful weight control. To help categorise the available options, Dr Allan Kristal and his colleagues in Seattle have come up with a 4-factor method of reducing fat in the diet. They suggest:

1. *Exclusion*, or the elimination of certain foods or food preparation techniques:
   Examples:
   - Not putting butter or margarine on toast
   - Avoiding sausages or luncheon meats
   - Eating salads without mayonnaise or dressing
   - Avoiding fried foods
2. *Modification*, or altering foods to be lower in fat.
   Examples:
   - Trimming fat off meat
   - Grilling rather than frying
   - Skimming fat off soups
   - Draining fat off cooked mince

3. *Substitution*, using reduced-fat or low-fat varieties of regular foods.
   Examples:
   - Choosing reduced-fat cheeses
   - Having skim milk instead of full-cream milk
   - Using lean mince
   - Eating reduced-fat ice cream
4. *Replacement*, or changing to new foods or ingredients.
   Examples:
   - Swapping lemon juice for salad dressing
   - Eating yoghurt instead of ice cream
   - Having fruit rather than a piece of cake
   - Basting meats with vegetable stock, not oil

10.   Break the fat addiction

Research from the Monell Chemical Senses Centre in Philadelphia has shown that cutting back on fat can reduce the pleasure of fatty foods. Scientists experimented with three groups of people: one group eating a normal, generally high-fat diet, a second on a fat-restricted diet and a third using low-fat substitutes for fatty foods in a normal diet.

Cutting back on fat can reduce the pleasure of fatty foods.

The groups were tested on their pleasure ratings of a range of foods during the 12 weeks they were on the diet and again 12 weeks after it finished. At the end of the initial period the researchers found a decrease in 'hedonic' ratings, or the degree of appeal of fatty foods, in the two groups with restricted fat intake. They also noticed a decrease in overall calorie intake, and a decrease in body weight in these groups compared to the normal diet group.

At the end of the post-test period (12 weeks later) the intake of fats and expressed satisfaction with fatty foods was still low in the low-fat diet group, but not in the group using low-fat replacement foods. The indications from this are that while fats might be addictive and may help increase the total calorie intake in the diet, restricting their use can break the addictiveness.

11. Don't cut out all fats—some are very healthy!

Unfortunately the message to reduce fat can be taken as 'all fats are bad'. But this is certainly not the case. A minimum amount of fat is needed to supply the body with essential fatty acids, which make nerve cells and hormones and help transport and absorb the fat-soluble vitamins A, D, E and K.

Scientists are also accumulating evidence which suggests that some fats are in fact beneficial in combating problems like heart disease and some cancers. The latest on the fish oils story provides a good example.

A study of people with heart disease in Seattle showed that people who eat at least one meal per week of fish had about half the risk of a heart attack as those who didn't eat fish. If true, the reason is likely to be that fish oils seem to make the blood less clottable and sticky. They may also make the heart muscle more stable and less prone to the type of abnormal rhythm which can lead to a cardiac arrest.

The Seattle study is one of many indicating benefits from regularly eating fish rich in omega-3 polyunsaturated fats. A practical recommendation for health is to aim for at least two fish meals a week.

Oils or spreads made from olive oil or canola oil also get the thumbs up from health authorities. If you use added fat, these are the oils of choice. While olive oil is over three-quarters mono-unsaturated fatty acids, canola oil has a significant omega-3 content. A recent addition to the market, Sunola oil, has the largest mono-unsaturated fat content at 85%.

The effects of these on health may be varied. The effects of their overconsumption on body weight, however, are likely to be more consistent (with the possible exception of fish oils), because all fats and oils have the equivalent of 9 kcals/g.

12.   Don't cut the fat for toddlers

Reduced-fat eating is now recommended for adults and adolescents. Diets low in fat, on the other hand, can compromise the growth of important nerve tissue in younger children.

Speaking at the 6th European Conference on Obesity in Copenhagen in 1995, Dr Michelle Rolland-Cachera, from L'Hôpital St Lazare in Paris, claimed there could be a decrease in growth potential with a limited intake of fat in the diet in young children. Infants in the early years require a high level of fat for their high energy needs, as well as for the myelination, or 'coating', of nerve fibres. Breast milk caters for this with a fat content of around 50%.

A low fat intake should be avoided in the early childhood years to guarantee optimal growth.

Thus a high fat intake is not always a bad thing, according to Dr Rolland-Cachera. In fact, a low fat intake should be avoided in the early childhood years to guarantee optimal growth.

13. Cut out (or at least cut back on) butter and margarine

Spreads such as butter and margarine have become popular more for social reasons than anything else. Some cultures don't bother with spreads at all. As a result they don't take in the high amounts of fat that come with the regular spreads we use on bread and toast.

One reasonable serving of butter or margarine on a slice of bread is the equivalent of around 5 g. As about 80% of this is fat (in the case of both butter and margarine—it's just that the type of fat is different), this means you're adding about 4 g of fat or 36 kcals of energy to every piece of bread you eat. If you consider that you might take in around 8–10 slices per day (including sandwiches, which have 2 slices), this amounts to 32–40 g of fat, or 288–360 kcals of energy—or about 10% of the daily energy intake!

Toast is even more of a worry because spreads tend to sink into hot toast. With butter in particular, this usually means that you have to have more to give you that 'lacquered' effect. You could wind up with the equivalent of about half a kilo of fat every 10 days—just through the spreads under your Vegemite or marmalade! Going off, or at least reducing spreads, whether butter or margarine, is a good way of stripping off the fat, without too much hardship.

14. Eat foods that satisfy satiety, not satiation

Satiation is the feeling of fullness at a meal; *satiety* is satisfaction some time later. Fatty foods have a low level of satiation, but a high level of satiety. This means that you can eat more fatty food during a meal without feeling full. (Have you noticed that it's always possible to slip in some extra chocolate, or a fatty dessert, afterward?) Satiety is generally higher later after a meal of fatty foods, but this is too late to stop eating more at the time.

High-carbohydrate and fibre-rich foods, on the other hand, have a high satiation value as well as a relatively high satiety value. This means that less (in terms of calories) is likely to be eaten at one time, because you're more likely to feel full. The implication is that a meal high in carbohydrate and fibre is likely to leave you feeling less hungry for a longer period as well as resulting in less energy being taken in, than a meal high in fat.

15.   Choose foods that fill you up

Foods are generally rated on their nutrient value—fat, carbohydrate or protein—with those trying to lose weight often recommended to cut back on fats or carbohydrates.

A new food index has recently been developed which suggests that this may not have the best practical value. The measure, called a 'satiety index', was developed by Dr Susanna Holt from the CSIRO in Sydney. It's expected to play a significant role in future weight loss and diabetes control programs.

As part of her research, Dr Holt fed a number of different foods to a group of people, then rated how satisfied they felt—their level of satiety—every 15 minutes over a 2-hour period. She then compared how much each ate after this period when allowed free access to food.

Dr Holt compared the satiety ratings of each food to bread, which was given a satiety index (SI) score of 100. The foods found to be highest on the SI score were not those that are craved most. In fact, foods high in fat (which also have the highest energy value) often have the lowest SI, meaning they're not really filling, even though they may be very tasty. The likely outcome? You feel like more.

THE SATIETY LEVEL OF DIFFERENT FOODS

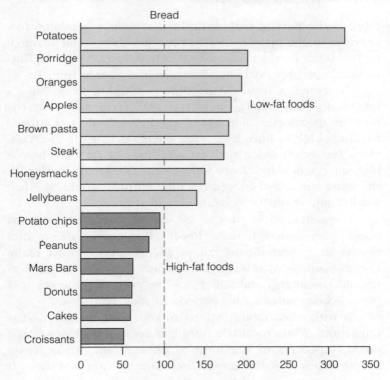

One of the highest SI scores found so far in the foods studied is for boiled potatoes (average SI = 323). Other carbohydrates, like porridge, fruit, pasta and even jellybeans, also rated highly (see table above). Croissants, which are high in fat, have the lowest SI so far (SI = 47), possibly explaining why that rich, Sunday morning breakfast leaves you hungry for more.

In contrast to fat, the protein, fibre and water contents of a food tend to increase its fillingness. Sugar doesn't seem to pose as much of a problem as fat, suggesting that satisfying a craving with sweets might be better than with fats.

16.   Fill up on fibre

Fibre is the part of carbohydrate that resists breakdown by enzymes in the intestine. Most fibre passes straight through to the large bowel ready for excretion in the faeces. Thus you can eat fibre without absorbing the energy from it.

The benefits from eating fibre-containing foods have a lot to do with 'energy density'. This term refers to the number of calories in a given weight of food. Many foods naturally high in fibre have a low energy density. In contrast, many fast foods laden with fat and little or no fibre have a high energy density. If you were to eat two meals, both with the same amount of energy, the high-fat meal would be much smaller and could be consumed a lot faster.

A recent review of the effects of energy density on obesity concluded that 'a low-fat, low-energy dense diet results in a spontaneous fall in energy intake whilst maintaining feelings of satiety'. This means that you can eat less fat and less energy and still avoid the 'perpetual hunger that often accompanies active periods of food restriction'.

As with most modifications to your diet, moderation is important. While too little fibre can cause constipation, too much, especially in the form of wheat bran, can decrease the absorption of the important minerals iron and zinc. It can also make you a little unpleasant to be around—if you get the drift! A target intake of around 30–40 grams of fibre a day is what you should be aiming for.

17.   Choose low glycaemic index foods

Because of their more complex structure, starches are more slowly digested than sugars. So it's been thought that these would be more beneficial in dealing with a disease such as diabetes, and for weight loss. But recently it's been shown that digestion and metabolism is not that simple. Some carbohydrates are not just broken down according to their simple or complex nature. Hence, another measure has been developed to explain this.

The Glycaemic Index (GI) is a method of classifying the glycaemic (i.e. blood sugar) response to carbohydrate-rich foods. Put another way, it's a measure of how quickly carbohydrate reaches the bloodstream. Foods can be tested and ranked out of 100 according to a measure of their GI, a bit like the satiety index (SI) discussed in Tips 14 and 15. Foods closer to 100 are more quickly digested, so foods with a lower GI should be preferred.

It doesn't necessarily follow that all sweet sugary foods will be quickly absorbed and therefore have a high GI. It's much more complex than this and depends on a number of characteristics of the food consumed. For example:

- Glucose (GI = 100) has a higher GI than fructose (GI = 20). Temperate fruits (e.g. apples, pears, oranges) have a higher fructose content than tropical fruits (eg. watermelon, rockmelon, mangoes).
- The ratio of two types of starches (amylose:amylopectin) can affect the GI of foods. Amylopectin is more easily digested than amylose. Therefore, foods such as legumes, with a high amylose:amylopectin ratio, have a lower GI than rice, which has a higher amylopectin content.
- Processing can increase the GI of a food. Wholemeal bread, where the grains have been ground down and incorporated into the dough, is more quickly digested (and hence has a higher GI) than a wholegrain rye bread, where the grains are still intact.
- Soluble fibre can decrease the rate of absorption of glucose and hence decrease GI. Fibre supplements have not been found to have the same effect because the fibre is not packaged into the food.
- Large amounts of fat can slow down digestion. While this results in a low GI for foods that contain both carbohydrate and fat (e.g. ice cream), the fat content should take first priority when making food selections.

Low GI foods are scored below 55, intermediate from 55 to 70, and high above 70. You can combine a high and low GI food to produce an intermediate GI meal. The use of low GI foods can be a useful addition to a reduced-fat, high-fibre eating plan.

GLYCAEMIC INDEX OF SOME SELECTED FOODS
Foods with a lower GI are likely to be better for effective weight control

Breads

Bagel	72	Croissant	67
Crumpet	69	Fruit loaf (white)	47
Mixed grain bread (av.)	45	Rye bread	50
White bread (av.)	70	Wholemeal (av.)	77

Breakfast cereals

Kellogg's All-Bran™	30	Sanitarium Weet-Bix™	75
Kellogg's Cornflakes™	77	Kellogg's Nutrigrain™	66
Kellogg's Sustain™	68	Kellogg's Mini-Wheats™	58
Muesli—untoasted	56	Porridge	42

Grains/pasta

Buckwheat	54	Noodles— instant	47
Rice — Calrose	83	Pasta — egg fettuccine	32
— Basmati	58	— ravioli (meat)	39
— brown	76	— spaghetti (av.)	41

Biscuits/cakes

Puffed Crispbread	81	Ryvita	69
Water Cracker	78	Arrowroot	69
Shredded Wheatmeal	62	Shortbread	64
Apple muffin	44	Sponge cake	46

Vegetables

Carrots	49	Parsnip	97
Potato — baked (av.)	85	Sweet potato	54
— new (av.)	62	Peas (green)	48
— pontiac	56	Sweet corn	55

Legumes			
Baked beans (av.)	48	Broad beans (av.)	79
Butter beans (av.)	31	Chick peas (av.)	33
Kidney beans (av.)	27	Soya beans (av.)	18
Fruit			
Banana (av.)	53	Cherries	22
Grapefruit	25	Grapes	43
Mango	55	Orange (av.)	43
Snacks			
Corn chips	72	Peanuts	14
Popcorn	55	Potato crisps	54
Dairy foods			
Milk — whole (av.)	27	Yoghurt (flav, low fat)	33
— skim	32	Ice cream (av.)	61

18. Put (resistant) starch back on the menu

Once thought to be a main cause of obesity, starchy foods are now thought to have just the opposite effect. But not all starches are the same, says Professor Alison Stephens, an expert in carbohydrate metabolism from the University of Satkatchewan in Canada. 'The re-emergence of starchy foods, (or non-fibre complex carbohydrates) and their influence in health is making the interest in fibre a little old fashioned', says Stephens.

Recently, attention has turned to a form of starch in foods called 'resistant', because this is not easily digested in the intestine. Raw potato and green banana contain the best (although slightly unpalatable) versions of this starch, and research comparing digestion of these has shown that not only do they add less calories to the diet, they appear to cause an increase in fat use instead of glucose use by the body.

Researchers from the prestigious Centre for Food Research in Denmark suggest that resistant starches may have an effect on fat-burning similar to a lack of food being eaten, because the food is not digested quickly to be burned as energy, resulting in fat being used instead. They could also have major benefits for diabetics and sufferers of other metabolic disorders. The recently introduced high-fibre white breads are a good source of resistant starch. There's more to come on these foods.

19.   Eat more fruit and veg

For years, health authorities have been encouraging us to eat more fruits and vegetables. The CSIRO Division of Human Nutrition in Adelaide, for example, recommends at least 3 serves of fruit and 4 serves of vegetables each day for health and weight control.

Vegetables have the lowest energy density of all the food groups. The average carrot provides only 24 kcal with 3 grams of fibre and no fat. Fruit contains a little more energy from natural sugars, mostly fructose.

Contrary to what some people think, bananas have very little fat (less than one-fifth of a gram). The odd fruit out is avocado. Munching on several avocados a day (about 40 grams per avocado) will add significantly to fat intake— even though the fat is healthy, mono-unsaturated fat. However, using avocado as a sandwich spread instead of margarine is a good way to cut back on unhealthy fat (see Tip 13).

If this were not enough, the increasing volume of scientific evidence linking fruit and vegetable consumption to reduced risk of various cancers is another plus for eating extra fruit and veg.

20. Eat the fruit rather than drink the juice

If you've been drinking a glass of fruit juice at breakfast for longer than you can remember, you might be a bit concerned after reading this headline. Well, don't be. But do take into consideration some of the waist-wise advantages of whole fruit over juice. As it takes around 500 g of fruit to make a cup of fruit juice, the sugar (and therefore energy) value of the juice becomes highly concentrated, and very easy to consume. On the other hand it's quite filling to eat the whole fruit which made it up.

> **Don't drink anything you can eat whole (with the possible exception of cow's milk!)**

Dietary fats are always the first priority for cutbacks in a weight control plan. After this, it's a good idea to check for excessive sugar. If you're drinking a litre of orange juice a day, sugar can add up and may need to be considered. For that reason a good principle is 'don't drink anything you can eat whole (with the possible exception of cow's milk!)'.

If you can't live without your juice in the morning, at least make sure you spend some energy—juice it by hand!

21. Make breakfast a priority

Physiologically speaking, it's easy to see why eating carbohydrate shortly after rising is a good way to go (figuratively, too!). Blood glucose levels fall overnight and without an early 'recharge' can drop further as the day progresses.

People who miss breakfast have the potential to get very hungry, very quickly. This intense feeling of hunger can then compromise wise food choices and lead to over-consumption of fatty foods.

High-fibre breakfast cereals have been found to delay the onset of hunger for longer periods than cereals with a lower fibre content. Getting more fibre from breakfast cereals has also been associated with choosing better sources of fibre during the day. Add to this the findings that breakfast eaters have a lower fat intake, smoke less and get more vitamin C, and you can appreciate why having breakfast is an integral part of a healthy lifestyle and weight control program.

22.   Don't go too long without eating

Hunger does not promote rational food choice. All good intentions go out the window when hunger calls. The usual time for this in human beings is around four hours after the last intake of food, so a basic rule is not to go for longer than about four hours without something (healthy) to eat.

One way of personally assessing the level of hunger, with a view to decreasing unnecessary eating, is to rate hunger on a scale such as that shown in the box below. Experiencing extreme ratings on the scale should be avoided, whether going without food (ravenous) or eating too much food (beyond full—feeling ill). A quick self-assessment should identify the causes of any hunger. Is it a genuine need for food or just a passing whim?

**Don't go for longer than
about 4 hours without
something (healthy) to eat.**

Subjective hunger scale
8. Beyond full—feeling ill
7. Very full
6. Slightly full
5. Feeling satisfied
4. No hunger
3. Slightly hungry
2. Hungry
1. Ravenous

23.   Find out where fat hides

When something looks and feels fatty, chances are it is. But today there's a huge selection of processed foods which have varying appearances and textures. Studies suggest that identification of fat content is more difficult in many of these foods.

Consumer research recently carried out by the Australian Dairy Corporation, for example, compared the actual fat content of various foods with consumers' knowledge of fat. Interestingly, estimated levels of fat in food were higher than the actual content for a range of fatty foods such as chips (52% perceived, compared to 32% actual), meat pies (45% to 14%) and sausages (47% to 17%), but lower on some other products like popcorn (consumers thought 20% compared to 25%).

Another study discovered that people commonly misclassify a number of foods. Again, consumers were asked to estimate the fat content of various foods. For some foods they dramatically under-estimated it, while for others it was over-estimated. Foods commonly misclassified as being higher in fat included potatoes, spaghetti, baked beans and beer. Those foods incorrectly perceived to be lower in fat included chicken with the skin, sardines, cheese and peanuts. Almost 70% of subjects thought that margarine was

lower in fat than butter. These findings underpin the importance of recognising the fat content of foods.

24. Check your figures

Selecting foods for fat content is becoming easier as more
food manufacturers put nutrition information panels on
their products. From a dietary fat perspective the most
important number is the amount of fat in grams per 100 g—
the lower the better. For those who need a guideline, try
choosing foods with less than 10 g fat per 100 g of food.
The box below shows a comparison of information for two
foods. Food 1 represents a packet of potato crisps, whereas
food 2 represents a packet of oven-baked pretzels. There's
a big difference in fat content, and it's obvious the pretzel
would be the better choice for a savoury snack.

SAMPLE NUTRITION INFORMATION PANEL		
	Food 1	*Food 2*
Servings per pack	Per 100 g	Per 100 g
Serving size	50 g	30 g
Energy	2290 kJ	1620 kJ
Protein	6.1 g	10 g
Fat	37.1 g	3 g
Carbohydrate		
Total	51.0 g	81.1 g
Sugars	0.4 g	4.0 g
Dietary fibre	5.6 g	5.5 g
Sodium	1600 mg	670 mg
Potassium	965 mg	1230 mg
Cholesterol	0 mg	0 mg

This arbitrary cut-off of 10 g/100 g needs to be flexible,
especially in the case of cheese, where the many reduced-fat
varieties still have around 24 g fat per 100 g. It's also
important to check that the serving size quoted on the pack

is realistic. For example, a 200 ml tub of regular yoghurt has about 8 g of fat. If you eat half a litre (which is reasonable), you'll take in 20 g of fat.

Where ingredient quantities are not given, manufacturers are required by law to name the ingredients in a product, listed in order of decreasing volume. To get around listing fat high on the ingredient list, some manufacturers show it as individual fats, which are less by volume. A general principle is to avoid foods where fats constitute any of the first three ingredients.

Fats can go under many names. A list of the common ones appears in the box.

COMMON NAMES FOR FATS ON FOOD LABELS

Lard, animal fat, animal shortening, coconut oil, palm oil, vegetable oil, butterfat, whole milk solids, copha, tallow, chocolate, chocolate chips, shortening, margarine, cocoa butter.

---

25. Watch out for fat–sugar combinations

Fats in foods are more of a concern than sugars for weight gain. But a combination of the two may become even more of a concern. There are a couple of reasons for this.

First, the fat–sugar combination makes it easier to get the food into your mouth. A study of 1700 women carried out in England found that the main risk from sugar in the diet is that it's used to make high-fat products like cakes, biscuits and chocolate more palatable. The research showed that most of the sugar eaten by these people was not 'added sugar' but 'hidden sugar' in processed foods. The sweet, fatty foods they ate tended to be eaten at the expense of fruit and vegetables.

Once inside the body this bliss-point mixture may

facilitate greater fat storage. Studies have recently been carried out on fat disappearance rates, or the rate at which fats in foods are used up in the body as energy. These show that after eating fatty, sugary foods, like ice cream, blood fats in the form of triglycerides are slower to disappear from the bloodstream than after eating either cream alone or sugar alone.

This suggests that the body is likely to store fat more readily if food fats are accompanied by sugars. Other research has shown a similar effect with a fat/alcohol combination. The time sequence of eating these is, however, unknown. So while the discerning waist watcher should look out for fat, avoiding its combination with either alcohol or sugar is probably even more important.

26. Avoid a low-fat overload

You're doing the right thing by choosing foods with less fat. But does this help you to reduce overall fat and energy intake? Some low- or no-fat yoghurts, ice creams and cakes can still contain a considerable amount of sugar. There's also the possibility of eating more so-called 'bad' foods because you've been 'good' earlier in the day. In these cases a low-fat label doesn't provide a licence to overeat—a belief that until recently was only supported by anecdotal evidence.

To analyse the phenomenon, two researchers at Penn State University conducted a study to find out whether information on the fat content of foods influenced subsequent food and overall energy intake. Forty-eight non-dieting women were given 350 grams of three different raspberry yoghurts to eat before lunch. They were low-fat, low-calorie (3 g fat/161 kcal), low-fat, high-calorie (2 g fat/357 kcal) and high-fat, high-calorie (26 g fat/357 kcal). The subjects didn't know which yoghurt they were given to eat, unless a label was attached. Lunch was a buffet style which they ate 30 minutes after eating the yoghurt.

Not surprisingly, the women who ate the yoghurt labelled low-fat consumed more energy at lunch than they did after eating one labelled high-fat. The effect was even noticed at dinner that evening—even though they consumed the same actual amount of energy from each yoghurt. This suggests a need for a greater awareness of how we go about balancing the reduced-fat foods we eat. If the consumption of low-fat foods is negated by eating more sugar or more fatty foods later, it will be hard to notice any long-term benefits.

27. Become aware of when you eat high-fat foods during the day

Rather than watching fat intake all day, there may be key times to be more conscious of what you eat. Research at the National Institutes of Health in Maryland in the United States shows that fat intake varies across the course of a day. Examining the food diaries of a large sample of women, researchers found that most have a very controlled fat intake early in the day. Even those women who have a high daily fat intake apparently eat less of it at the morning meal and at snacks, but then eat more fat than lower fat eaters at lunch and dinner.

This implies that a low-fat breakfast can be easily achieved, whereas fat restriction at later meals can be more of a challenge. Focusing on the fat content of lunch or dinner may be a more productive strategy that could have significant (and livable) effects for some people.

28. Don't bother with food combining

The notion of combining or, more correctly, excluding, the combination of certain foods has a long history. First proposed in the 1920s by a medical graduate, the common claim is that the human body doesn't possess enough of the enzymes required to digest both protein and carbohydrate at the same time. Eating these together would thus overload the system.

If this biochemical claim were true (and it isn't), it would be an advantage for fat loss as some food would remain undigested and pass through the body without the energy being absorbed. But the human body is perfectly capable of dealing with any nutrients, be they protein, carbohydrate, fat or alcohol, all at the same time. If it wasn't, human beings wouldn't have evolved into what they are today. Those who are biochemically ignorant fail to recognise that the body has different enzymes specifically for each nutrient. One enzyme, pepsin, works on protein while a whole team of sugar enzymes goes to work on carbohydrate. Diets which promote an enzymatic benefit from separating nutrients or foods are misguided.

29. Avoid the dangers of popular diets

If we didn't know it before, a survey of 19 popular diets from women's magazines reported in the *Australian Journal of Nutrition and Dietetics* has found that none conform to both the national guidelines for nutritional health and the recommended dietary targets. The survey also showed that:

- The most popular diets contain an appropriate amount of energy from fat, but about half provide too little energy from carbohydrate
- Recommended fibre intake is too low in about one-third of commercial diets
- Iron intake was less than 70% of the recommended daily intake in up to half of the diets
- Nearly half of the diets assessed included no cereals, vegetables or dairy foods on some days, often limiting intake to only fruit.

The question, of course, becomes just what the women's magazines will use to sell copy once this information sinks in. Fortunately there's still the Royal Family—at least at the time of writing!

30.   Get smart with artificial sweeteners

The advent of artificial sweeteners was supposed to be a boon to those watching their waistlines. But claims in the popular media that these may increase appetite, and therefore food consumption, have led some consumers to question their usefulness for reducing energy intake.

To investigate these claims, Dr Adam Drewnowski, a renowned expert in the field from the University of Michigan, has reviewed all the research in the area. He concludes 'there is no evidence that the addition of an intense sweetener to a plain stimulus promotes appetite or results in increased food consumption during some later meal'.

Drewnowski's analysis is a revelation of how misinformation in the health area is spread. Most claims that intense sweeteners promote hunger and increase food consumption have been based largely on two published pieces of research. The first, a letter to the *Lancet*, claimed that the use of aspartame (a commonly used sweetener) increased the motivation to eat. The second report, from a reputable laboratory in the United Kingdom, claimed to show an increase in food consumption later in the day after sweetener use. Although this was reported widely, later research failed to replicate the results.

Drewnowski's conclusion, based on a careful review of all the research on the subject, is that hunger is more affected by the type and volume of food eaten than by the sweetness or calorie density of the food. Sweeteners do not appear to influence appetite or food consumption.

There's also the question of whether sweeteners actually help fat loss. Using artificially sweetened foods does appear to be more effective than naturally sweetening products with sucrose. But few long-term studies have compared sweetened foods in an eating plan with non-sweetened alternatives. One such study, reported in the journal *Appetite* in 1988, did show that people using sweeteners had a better long-term maintenance of weight loss. Your own research may provide the best guide.

31.   Outsmart cravings

The way to a man's heart, it's said, is through his stomach. But if you're thinking of getting there with chocolate, think again. A good hunk of steak might do the trick better.

Research on food cravings is now beginning to uncover why a man feels he must have a steak when all a woman wants is chocolate. Cravings, for people eating normally, it seems, are not based on nutritional needs, but are probably hormonal or psychological in origin. How else can it be explained that young pre-menopausal women crave fat, sugar and carbohydrates, whereas post-menopausal women, whose female hormonal status has changed, have cravings more akin to a man's?

Although studies are yet to prove this idea, there is good evidence to show that the food cravings of men and women are different. According to Dr Harvey Weingarten of McMaster University in Canada, 97% of young women he sampled in a large study on food cravings claim to have unexplained midnight urges for particular foods. This occurred in only 67% of men. These findings are discussed in a book called *Why Women Need Chocolate*, by dietitian Debra Waterhouse. She claims that men crave meat because they need protein for muscle. Meanwhile, Dr Adam Drewnowski, an expert in taste preferences, has shown that many foods high on the female preference list are a mixture of fat and sugar. If you have an overwhelming craving for something sweet, think sweet but not fatty. Having jelly babies instead of chocolate may not always work, but when you're done eating jelly babies, you haven't eaten any fat.

Savoury cravings may need to be satisfied by that 'meaty' flavour—just make sure it's lean.

32. Beware of the eye–mouth gap

Ask someone what they ate yesterday and chances are they'll under-estimate the amount. This phenomenon, called the 'eye-mouth gap', has been the glitch in many studies which have set out to examine just how much fat people eat.

People systematically understate the amounts of all nutrients they're eating, but they particularly under-report fat and carbohydrates.

Danish researchers asked middle-aged men and women about their exercise and eating habits and then compared their reported food intake with actual biological measures.

The results showed that people systematically understate the amounts of all nutrients they're eating, but particularly under-report fat and carbohydrates. Other work has suggested that the whole foods being understated tend to be the snack and fast food items.

Experts in this type of research believe that under-reporting is not a deliberate deception, but the unconscious result of social pressures to which everyone appears to be susceptible to varying degrees. The important thing is to be aware of how much food you put on your plate. An eating diary might come in handy, at least for a while, to check serving sizes and those times when memory fails.

33.   Add a little spice to your food

The idea that spicy foods may have some benefit in fat loss was first put to the test by scientists in 1985. In an experiment using a variety of different spicy foods, it was found that metabolic rate was increased, thereby resulting in an increase in energy use over a 24 hour period. Naturally this created a lot of interest in the weight control industry, although for many years the results couldn't be replicated. Some research carried out at the University of Tasmania in the early 1990s, however, may put the whole idea back on the waist watchers' table. Dr Eric Colquhoun and his colleagues found that:

- Different foods have different levels of the main spice ingredient associated with metabolic increases, and
- There has to be a prolonged use of the right type of spice to get any metabolic benefits.

According to Dr Colquhoun, one ingredient common to spices like peppers and chillies could be responsible for most of the fat-burning effect. The ingredient is called capsaicin. The Tasmanian group found that if capsaicin was injected into a rat, oxygen consumption was increased to the large muscles, meaning an increase in energy being used up, and ultimately therefore a decrease in body fat.

However, the Tasmanian researchers also found that the amount of capsaicin varied from around 47% in Tabasco sauce to around 5% in other types of chilli sauces. It's difficult therefore to make a global statement about the benefits of spices without knowing their natural constituents.

Colquhoun's group also found that oxygen consumption in rat tissue didn't increase until some days after the introduction of spicy foods into the bloodstream, but then led to a gradual increase in metabolism.

The research has re-opened the issue of spicy foods and weight control. While a metabolic boost should be seen as a possible bonus, spicy flavours can improve the taste of

KING MIDAS' BROTHER EFRAM, WHO UNFORTUNATELY TURNED EVERYTHING HE TOUCHED TO FAT.

low-fat food. For those complaining of dietary blandness, give them some of the hot stuff.

34. Go for something unfamiliar

Dietary-induced thermogenesis is the term given to energy used up (and given off as heat) following the digestion of food. This is known to form a significant part of daily energy use (around 15–20%). Any increase in thermogenesis may be beneficial for fat loss.

A possible way of doing this was hinted at in European research testing thermogenesis in a group of women given familiar and unfamiliar foods. Diet-induced thermogenesis during the first serving of a meal consisting of unfamiliar food was found to be significantly higher than when familiar foods were eaten. Familiarity—in metabolic terms—may breed content. Try some unfamiliar foods to make the body work harder.

35.   Make the most of caffeine

It's well known that caffeine, as in coffee, can have a stimulatory effect in many people. Several studies have now also shown that this is translated into thermogenesis—it can help increase metabolic rate. Some studies show an increase in metabolism of 7–22% in lean people, according to the amount of coffee consumed.

There's also evidence that caffeine increases fat burning and helps to spare carbohydrate as a fuel. For that reason it's used by endurance athletes in long distance events. For the same reason moderate coffee consumption (i.e. 3–4 cups daily) has been promoted as an aid for those wanting to lose extra body fat.

Research from Switzerland, however, suggests that the effect of caffeine may not be as great in those people who need it most. Measuring lean and obese people in a metabolic chamber over 24 hours, researchers found that the effects of caffeine were blunted in those regarded as obese. Although there still was some effect, it tended to decrease with the level of body fat.

The researchers suggest that for various physiological reasons, obesity decreases the ability to metabolise caffeine, resulting in a less significant effect. There may still be a small effect, however, which can at least justify not cutting caffeine out of a rational eating plan.

36.   Check your level of dietary restraint

At first glance you may be excused for thinking that restrained eating—being careful about what you eat—would be a positive way of keeping your weight down. But the emergence of scientific studies on eating disorders suggests that the connection isn't so clear.

Restrained eaters count calories, don't finish meals to the point of satisfying hunger, choose low-calorie food, avoid sweets and fats and are permanently cautious about their weight and eating behaviour. They're generally female and can be identified by their level of cognitive or mental control during eating. Ironically, obese women are more likely to be restrained eaters than the non-obese.

So if restrained eating means restricting food intake, and if reduced food intake reduces body fat, what's going wrong?

From recent research it appears that the degree of rigidity of restrained eating is a key factor. Those who have strict control over their eating can usually perform well until they are faced with a disturbance. Stress, conflict, depression or other personal problems can easily disrupt the pattern and, once it's disrupted, can cause total collapse.

According to German psychologist Dr Volker Pudel, who specialises in the psychology of obesity, self-imposed cognitive control only works as long as it's not violated. Once this happens, the whole system of self-control collapses; bingeing and over-eating occur as compensation, and the individual is likely to gain fat.

Restrained eaters who allow a greater flexibility in conditions they set themselves—parties, break-outs, etc.—are more likely to be able to cope with such setbacks. This flexibility, in contrast to a rigidity of approach, means that dietary glitches can be tolerated.

The implications of this are that flexibility in any eating plan is essential for long-term fat loss. Not only will rigid control reduce the effectiveness of a weight loss program, it's likely to increase weight gain.

37. If you enjoy a drink—don't give it up, just trade it off

Restrictive diets don't work because of the risk of rebound bingeing. Giving up alcohol can have a similar effect. If abstaining from the grog results in a psychological battle to stay off it, this can be counter-productive. You have to feel comfortable that any change is manageable.

When asked about adopting healthy habits, most men clearly indicate that they want as little upset to their current lifestyle as possible.

Rather than become non-drinkers, they'd prefer to do extra physical activity to burn off the energy from drinks. This makes sense, and allows a drink to be enjoyed even more when it's deserved.

How much is too much? The World Health Organisation has classified drinking levels. Consuming less than two standard drinks a day may pose no health risk. Daily consumption of more than two drinks for women and four for men can be potentially hazardous.

WHAT IS A STANDARD DRINK?

A standard drink is that amount of an alcoholic beverage which contains 10 grams of alcohol:

375 mL can of low alcohol beer
285 mL glass of regular beer
100 mL small glass of wine
60 mL glass of fortified wine
30 mL nip of spirits

---

38. Forget the 'beer belly'—concentrate on the 'beer + peanuts' or the 'beer + chips' belly

Contrary to popular opinion, there's no such thing as a beer belly. Alcohol *per se* doesn't make you fat. It's what goes with the alcohol that causes the problem. This evidence comes from a number of quarters: in the first place, there's good statistical information to show an inverse relationship between body weight and alcohol consumption in many countries. This is particularly so with females.

There's no such thing as a beer belly. Alcohol *per se* doesn't make you fat. It's what goes with the alcohol that causes the problem.

Secondly, alcohol is regarded as a toxin, and as such is thought to be metabolised by the body for energy, lost as heat, or used as a fuel of first priority. Alcohol, like carbohydrate, seems to be used before fats in the energy system.

Finally, research substituting alcohol energy for carbohydrates or fats has generally shown a lower increase in body weight over time, thus supporting the notion that alcohol is generally used up as energy rather than stored as fat.

If alcohol is combined with fatty foods, however, the alcohol will be used as energy and the fats stored in the fat cells. Thus, it's probably not the alcohol that causes the beer belly, but the chips, peanuts and other fatty foods consumed with it. If you cut out the fats, it's more likely that you'll cut out the beer belly—even without cutting out the beer.

39.   Dietary fat: don't go too low too quickly

Reduction of dietary fat is an essential anti-obesity strategy. But how far can you cut back on fat before the body gets smart and figures out some form of dietary compensation? Researchers at the University of Leeds have gone part of the way to answering this question.

These scientists had previously found that a fat reduction from 40% to 30% of daily energy intake caused no physiological or behavioural responses (i.e. the body didn't seem to miss the fat at all). Following this they conducted another experiment to look at the effects of a more severe reduction in fat intake.

In a covert feeding study subjects participated in two 2-day test sessions. On day one of the first test, they ate meals containing 32% energy as fat (a moderate reduction from the average 38% consumed in Britain). On day one of the second test, they ate meals containing only 20% energy as fat. On day two of both tests, the subjects were allowed to eat *ad libitum* and their food intake was monitored. (To ensure that they were unaware of any manipulation, and to eliminate sensory influences, a fat substitute was used to produce the fat reductions in the second test.)

In this experiment a 74% compensation in energy intake occurred the day after using the fat substitute. The group was also tested on their hunger ratings. On the day of the fat substitution, subjects were more hungry in the afternoon and the next morning they were still hungry. It appeared that the sudden drop in fat intake to well below their habitual intake stimulated a biobehavioural response to eat more.

The indications from this are that while people may be able to successfully handle fat reductions from 40% to 30% of food energy, more drastic reductions in dietary fat, where energy intake also falls, may thwart dietary adherence. It also shows that the heavy use of fat substitutes may not be as effective if a hunger response is triggered. Whether or not a gradual decrease in fat over a number of weeks can reduce any compensation remains to be tested.

40. Fat substitutes—watch this space

In 1990, 10% of food products were labelled either low-fat or no-fat, obviously capitalising on market demand. But because fat is tasty, the prize awaits whoever develops the best no-fat, fat-tasting substitute. Basically, four types of fat substitutes are currently available:

- Protein-based fat substitutes are usually made from milk and/or egg white proteins, sugar, pectin and citric acid (e.g. Simplesse). They have the disadvantage of being heat sensitive and therefore cannot be used in cooking.
- Carbohydrate-based fat substitutes can be in either digestible or indigestible form, and are usually made from starches. They feel like oil in the mouth because of their ability to form heat-stable gels. However, as with protein-based products, they can't be used for cooking.
- Fat-based fat substitutes are modified-fat alternatives to the fat they replace, and although they still provide calories can be effective in small amounts. They're mostly used in soft confectionery and can reduce the calorie content of baked and filled dairy products, but probably do not satisfy the fatty craving.
- Synthetic non-calorie fat substitutes are probably the most extensively studied type at the moment, with big promises being held out for Olestra, which was approved in the United States in 1996. The product tastes and behaves like fat but is not absorbed. It can also replace other edible oils and be used in cooking.

The big increase in fat substitutes has naturally led to concerns about safety. With standard food additives, testing is subject to a rigid set of experimental criteria where 100 times the normal quantity is fed to animals over an extended period. But unlike most food additives, which are only consumed in small quantities, fat substitutes could replace a substantial proportion of the diet for some people. Safety is therefore difficult to guarantee from animal research.

In all, there does appear to be potential in the diet for low-fat substitutes, but at the moment not all the information is in. It may be advisable to use low-fat substitutes with caution and to 'watch this space'.

41.   Keep protein levels high

Decreases in metabolism with decreases in food intake have been consistently shown to be from 10–20%, and a big drop can occur even in the first 24 hours of an energy-restricted diet. This is likely to have a big effect on total energy expenditure and hence on weight loss. It's a normal physiological response to sudden changes in body mass designed to protect against starvation.

Recent research carried out at the Rowett Research Institute in Scotland suggests that maintaining protein intake while decreasing total energy may maintain muscle mass and thus protect metabolic rate. Studying a small group of men and women in a metabolic chamber, where energy expenditure can be accurately assessed, the researchers examined changes in metabolic rate with three 7-day diets using high protein, normal protein and high fat, and normal protein and high carbohydrate.

Each person was tested on each of the diets over a 7-day period with a 7-day 'wash-out' in between. Each of the diets contained a total of 1000 kcals multiplied by 1.4 times the metabolic rate of the individual. The high protein diet contained 36% protein compared to 15% in the other diets. The remaining 64% was divided equally between carbohydrate and fat. The high-carbohydrate diet had 53% carbohydrate and the high-fat diet 53% fat.

Although the diets were too short (7 days) to achieve any noticeable differences in body weight, there were big differences in metabolic rate. On high protein there was no decrease in metabolic rate, while there was a 3.5% decrease on the high-carbohydrate mix and a 5% decrease on high-fat mix. This amounted to an energy difference between the high protein and other diets of around 45 kcals a day. The reason for energy maintenance with high protein would appear to be the decrease in the proportion of lean body mass (muscle) lost with the diet, which then helps to maintain a high metabolism. A total of 45 kcals a day may not seem much, but could be significant over time because it may also help prevent further declines in metabolism.

The suggestion appears to be that in any energy restriction, particularly low fat for fat loss, protein levels should be kept high. Good sources of high-protein low-fat energy, such as seafood, beans or lentils, may be useful for this purpose.

42. If you like chips, make them low-fat

Potato chips are one of the most tempting morsels on any careful food eater's list. But they're also disastrous in terms of fat and energy content.

There are ways, however, of lowering the fat content and keeping the taste. Here are just some of them.

1. Use frozen chips, not thawed: Potato chips which are pre-cut and frozen form an instant crust when dropped in oil, thus minimising water loss and fat absorption. Thawed chips release more water into the surrounding oil, lower the oil temperature, and absorb more oil.

2. Cook at the right temperature: The best temperature for cooking lower-fat chips is between 180–185°C. Cooking chips at a lower temperature reduces the formation of the crust on the chip surface which reduces the excessive absorption of fat. Estimates suggest that 40% more fat is absorbed when the temperature is 10% lower than the recommended cooking temperature of 180–185°C. Cooking at excessively high temperatures, on the other hand, can change the nature of the oil and make it less healthy.

3. Use poly- or mono-unsaturated oils: The fat quality of

chips is affected by the type of oil in which they are cooked. Stable oils with a high level of mono-unsaturated fats, such as Sunola oil (from sunflowers), are known to be relatively stable and long lasting. Other apparently healthy choices, such as cottonseed oil and soybean-based oils, are less stable and more susceptible to undesirable changes under high temperature.

4. Maintain the quality of the oil: Older oil (or fat) is characterised by a darkness in colour and a tendency to smoke. Older oils inhibit the formation of the crust on the chip which reduces fat absorption. Oils should be discarded regularly, as continual heating can change their structure to include more trans-fatty acids.

5. Use the right type of chip: Absorption of fat in cooking is affected by the surface area of the chip. Because of its greater surface area, a crinkle cut chip is likely to absorb more fat and therefore have a higher fat content than a plain chip. Bigger chips also have less surface area to total volume than small, thin chips (French fries).

43.   Estimate how much food you really need

Determination of energy (food) requirements has long been a source of study. In 1996 a whole issue of the *European Journal of Clinical Nutrition* was devoted to a state-of-the-art seminar on the topic.

The first stage in estimating how much food you need is measuring resting metabolic rate (RMR). This is done through detailed and complicated laboratory analyses, or it can be estimated through formulae, such as those in Tip 3.

Even a 50 kg woman requires around 1220 kcals per day to balance metabolism in the resting state. Special calculations are then needed to estimate the extra requirements for physical activity carried out throughout the day. A table

indicating the energy required at different levels of exertion
is shown below:

ENERGY INTAKES REQUIRED AT
VARIOUS ACTIVITY LEVELS

Chair or bed-bound	RMR x 1.2
Seated with no option of moving and little exercise	RMR x 1.4–1.5
Seated work with requirement to move around but little strenuous exercise	RMR x 1.6–1.7
Standing work (e.g. housework, shop assistant)	RMR x 1.8–1.9
Strenuous work or highly active leisure	RMR x 2.0–2.4

44.   Beware the post-alcohol binge!

Although it's not well researched in the scientific literature,
there's abundant anecdotal evidence to suggest that the
craving for fats and sweets is increased after a night of
alcohol consumption. The reasons for this are not clear, nor
is it possible to say at this stage whether it can be controlled. An awareness of the problem might just help to
reduce its effects by helping you alter your post-alcohol
eating patterns—if this is an issue.

It's now well known that fats in foods are the big danger.
Sweets, without fats, don't seem to have the same potential
for body fat storage. Hence the post-alcohol craving might
be satisfied with sweet but low-fat foods, such as jellybeans,
jubes, meringues or dried fruits like dates or prunes.

There's no guarantee this will happen. But it just might
be worth a try to help you through these possible danger
periods.

2

EXERCISE

Ask anybody how to lose weight and they'll invariably answer 'diet and exercise'. We've seen in the previous chapter how the typical diet can be downright counter-productive. Now it might interest you to know that the usual approach to exercise is probably also wrong.

The standard idea about exercise is that you give until it hurts—the 'no pain, no gain' philosophy. Yet physiological research shows that this is not only incorrect, it may also be dangerous. Anyone carrying excess poundage is likely to also be a little unfit. And doing vigorous exercise when you're unfit can put extra pressure on the heart and bring on a potential heart attack.

More importantly, high-intensity exercise doesn't burn fat, it uses that other main energy source, glucose, from carbohydrate. In someone who's not very fit, high intensity is not very high. So any form of activity that's painful—or even somewhat uncomfortable—is not likely to optimally use up excess body fat in a fat person, even though it might do so in someone who is very fit.

The implications of this are that exercise doesn't have to be, and indeed shouldn't be, very vigorous for fat loss. Movement is about the most that's necessary. Because of increases in technology and effort-saving devices in modern society, nobody does much of this any more. It's this incidental movement which can add to the energy burned up during the course of a normal day. There are a number of simple ways of doing this, all discussed in the present chapter.

45. Don't worry about getting fit

Exercise carries the connotation of health. The big increases in obesity in recent years have concentrated attention on whether a reduction in body fat, rather than exercise *per se*, may be better for the average person, especially as there's a natural tendency to get fatter as you get older. Is it important to fight the increase, or simply to carry out some light activity daily?

Research carried out at the University of Maryland with middle aged and older men compared the benefits of aerobic exercise vs weight loss in altering risk factors for heart disease. Men aged 61 and older were given either a regular exercise program on cycles and treadmills 3 times a week, or instruction on how to cut down food intake. Results were compared with a control group who maintained their weight over the 9 months of the program.

Surprisingly, while those in the weight loss group lost about 10% of their body weight, they didn't increase their fitness, but still demonstrated improvements in blood pressure, blood fats and blood sugars. For those in the exercise only group, while there was an improvement in fitness there was no loss in weight, and also relatively little change in risk factors.

The researchers concluded that, at least in middle aged men, weight loss is more important than fitness in reducing risk factors. Those just carrying out an exercise program without reducing energy intake are less likely to see benefits than those changing their proportion of body fat.

46.   Increase your incidental activity

Captain Cook didn't need an aerobics instructor on board. And neither would we if we had to do what our forebears had to just to stay alive—chop the wood, catch a kangaroo, wash the clothes by hand etc. All this adds up to a decreased energy use in modern times which has been estimated to be around 800 kcals a day, or the equivalent of 1 lb of fat every 4 days!

Captain Cook didn't need an aerobics instructor on board. And neither would we if we had to do what our forebears had to just to stay alive.

How do you catch a kangaroo today? You don't (unless you want the animal rights lobby on your doorstep). But you can walk instead of driving the car, use stairs instead of escalators, not use technology where person-power can do the job, or even stand when you can sit. All of these incidental movements—and many more—can help burn the fat that's now not being burned because of the use of technology. Think incidental activity, and you need to worry less about exercise.

47.   Think of movement as an opportunity, not an inconvenience

In an age of technology, we're encouraged to think that we've 'made it' if we don't have to do anything through the day, if technology and hirelings can do everything for us.

But the human body is not ready for the technological revolution. The mindset that leads us to become totally inactive needs to be changed to one that appreciates, but does not idolatrise, technology. By regarding all forms of movement as an opportunity, rather than an inconvenience, the amount of total movement carried out during the day, and hence the amount of energy and ultimately fat burned up by the body, will be increased.

The human body is not ready for the technological revolution.

48.   Carry out small regular bouts of physical activity

Work with athletes has led scientists to think that exercise needs to be carried out in one session to get the best benefits. While this may be true for anyone wanting to increase their fitness level, it's now thought that it's not necessary for reducing fatness.

Research with obese women carried out at the University of Pittsburgh compared those walking for 4 bouts of 10 minutes a day over 3 months with those walking for one session of 40 minutes a day at the same intensity. The results showed that because the group carrying out the short bursts complied much more readily with the program, they tended to lose as much or more body weight over the test period. Perhaps unexpectedly, they also had a slightly better improvement in their cardiovascular fitness.

The results are almost certainly due to the fact that it's easier for big people to comply with a program of shorter exercise sessions. Frequent short bouts of movement therefore appear to be a better recommendation for long-term weight loss than longer, less frequent bouts.

**Frequent short bouts of
movement appear to be a
better recommendation for
long-term weight loss than
longer, less infrequent
bouts.**

49.   Don't over-estimate the role of fitness-type exercise in weight control

The scientific evidence for exercise in weight loss—particularly in very big people—is surprisingly equivocal. This could be because the *net* value of exercise has been over-estimated, say United States exercise specialists Glen and Arlene Blix.

Most estimates of the value of exercise are based on the amount of energy (calories) 'burned up' during the exercise. Jogging a mile, for example, will burn around 400 kJ. If 1 kg of fat is the equivalent of 32 000 kJ this means an extra mile a day would burn up 1 kg of fat in about 5 weeks.

But as the Blixes point out, this ignores the fact that if someone isn't jogging, they're doing something else. Even lying in bed requires energy. Hence it's the *net* energy used during exercise that should be considered, rather than the *gross* expenditure. If the alternative to jogging was walking around the house, about 200 kJ might be burned in the same period. So it would now take closer to 7.5 weeks to burn the extra kg of fat—and that makes it a less rosy proposition.

In addition to this, the amount of energy used up during exercise decreases with the amount of weight lost. Theoretically then, any loss in weight from exercise will tend to slow down the rate of weight loss that occurs from a similar amount of exercise in the future. In fact, Blix and Blix calculate that even if you walked 1000 miles, you'd only lose

3.53 lb of fat, rather than the 33 lb predicted by other equations!

While none of this discounts the value of regular exercise for fat loss, it does add a sobering note to the idea that a 30 minute aerobics class three times a week is the answer to your weight control problems. Regular, daily 'planned' and 'incidental' exercise needs to be a lifestyle activity for long-term weight control.

50.   Add planned daily activity to your routine

Changes in the way we live have meant reductions in the amount of physical activity that needs to be carried out daily to stay alive. Some of this can be compensated for by increases in incidental activity, as described in Tips 46 and 47. But modern society has also created a need for the institutionalisation of exercise.

To some extent this explains the rise of the fitness industry and the gym culture. Instead of getting a workout chopping wood or ploughing the fields, modern humans have been driven into the somewhat artificial environment of a gymnasium to get their exercise. While a gym may not be necessary, some form of planned activity during the day will help to compensate for effort not otherwise performed, and hence fat not otherwise burned.

Planning for an activity means taking time out of the daily routine. While this doesn't have to be all in one session (see Tip 48), it might require some restructuring of the social schedule.

51.   Go for distance, not speed

A legacy of the fitness tradition is that effort is important. The faster and harder an exercise is carried out, the greater the improvement in fitness. But as we've said, reducing fatness is different to increasing fitness. Body fat responds to total energy use. In a relatively fat, unfit person, intensive activity can result in blood sugars rather than fats being used as the fuel source. Setting a distance rather than a speed is therefore likely to be more productive for fat loss.

Walking a daily distance of 3–4 kilometres is generally accepted as appropriate for most people. This can be carried out at a leisurely pace, or even done as three or four bouts of 1 kilometre. The main thing is to make sure that it's done. An equivalent distance for cycling is around 15–20 km. You'll need to work out your own equivalents for other activities, like rowing or skiing.

52. Long and slow does the job

You may have always wanted to run a marathon (although goodness only knows why) but been turned off by all the heavy training involved. You might give an eye tooth to be fit and healthy, but can't stand the thought of getting out of breath. You might give an arm and a leg to lose weight, but are terrified of . . . well . . . losing an arm and a leg.

The good news is all these things may be possible—without busting a gut. This has been shown with novice marathon runners at the University of Northern Iowa. A total of 28 healthy males and 41 healthy females were trained (at the same intensity) either over 4 days a week or 6 days a week for 15 weeks before completing a marathon.

Surprisingly, those who trained for only 4 days a week were able to complete the event as quickly as those who trained over 6 days. They also lost as much body fat and had other similar improvements in markers of fitness, suggesting that, at least in novices, a high level of intense training is not necessary. The intensity of the training was also only moderate (i.e. 60–75% of maximum), suggesting benefits in terms of fat loss and fitness result from a lower intensity of exercise than is often recommended.

53. Only do planned exercise that you enjoy

It's important for weight control that any planned exercise program is able to be maintained for a lifetime. By definition, this is only likely to be done if it's enjoyable. While enjoment might not be expected on day 1, it should be apparent after several sessions whether you're going to enjoy an exercise enough to keep it up.

As movement, rather than any one particular type of exercise, is the key to long-term success, a regular planned exercise program should include those activities you like doing. Try several different types—walking, cycling, rowing, weight training—to help you make up your mind. Alternatively, you can vary your activity from day to day to get the maximum enjoyment.

54. Do different types of exercise

For successful weight loss, planned exercise needs to be carried out over a lifetime. One of the main constraints to this, for many people, is the boredom or staleness which can set in.

Varying the exercise routine—type, duration, location, time of the day—not only increases the prospects of enjoyment, it enhances the prospects of fat burning through *change* (see Tip 62). Change to the routine prevents the body from adapting to one particular form of activity and hence becoming too efficient at carrying it out. If adaption occurs, less energy, and therefore less fat, is used up carrying out the activity.

While specificity (i.e. carrying out the same activity regularly) is vital for athletes who are competing in a particular event, it's not necessary for fat loss. The main requirement for fat loss is the regular use of energy—any energy!

55.   Develop a regular exercise routine to *keep weight off* after you've lost it

The importance of exercise really comes to the fore in weight maintenance, rather than in the early stages of weight loss. Research has shown that over the long term, a lifestyle program with exercise built into it is much more likely to be effective. It helps burn energy (if done the right way). It may even help change eating patterns. Men in particular have been shown to eat more carbohydrate and less fat as a result of a regular planned exercise program. Relapse is also less likely in women who include exercise as a regular routine in maintenance.

> **Over the long term, a lifestyle program with exercise effort (i.e. movement) built into it is much more likely to be effective.**

For a big person then, the changes that are likely to have the greatest effect early in a fat-loss program are changes in food type (i.e. fat) combined with increases in incidental activity. More planned activity should be built into an ongoing program to prevent relapse and weight regain.

56.   Use a different measure of exercise intensity if you've been obese

When planning exercise for the obese, either traditional measures of % heart rate reserve (% HRR) or subjective measures of perceived rate of exertion (PRE) have been used to prescribe exercise intensity. While these measures have been found to be interchangeable in fit young individuals, the situation may be different in those who have lost substantial amounts of weight.

While % HRR is a good measure of aerobic capacity in the obese, a decrease in resting heart rate with fat loss makes it a less accurate measure with those who have lost weight. The margin of error could be as high as 10%. For this reason the more subjective PRE scales, where individuals rate their level of exertion on a 10 point scale (see below) are recommended as a more valid measure over the course of weight loss. A PRE score of 3–4 is regarded as optimal for ongoing fat loss.

PRE scale
 0 very, very weak
 1 very weak
 2 weak
 3 moderate
 4 somewhat strong
 5 strong
 6
 7 very strong
 8
 9
10 very, very strong (maximal effort)

57. Try weight training—but only if you're not very fat

There's controversy in the scientific literature about the use of weight training in fat loss. In theory, weights can help maintain lean body (muscle) mass and metabolic rate even while the body is losing fat. This would then assist in the decrease in body fat.

In practice, the obese or very overweight are generally concerned about their total body size, irrespective of their muscle-to-fat ratio. They're also likely to find it embarrassing and uncomfortable to lift weights. Hence, their time is probably more efficiently spent carrying out more aerobic-type activities such as walking.

On the other hand, for someone who doesn't have a lot of fat to lose, weight training can help maintain muscle which may otherwise be lost through food restriction (see Tip 2). The most effective form of weight training for this purpose is circuit training, or the use of relatively light weights with high repetitions (i.e. 15–20 reps).

58. Try this one—but only if you're very fit

Some extra active people have difficulty losing that extra half a kilo of fat—despite their high energy output. Why is this? Can anything be done?

The question has been partially answered by a study from the University of Limberg in the Netherlands, looking at the

PUMPING IRONS.

metabolism of fat in athletes who have over-trained and who are given a fat supplement as well as a carbohydrate supplement. The researchers found that depleting the body's carbohydrate stores—the opposite to carbohydrate loading as used by marathon runners and other endurance athletes—might decrease body fat, depending on the nutrient state at the time.

The scientists reduced the glycogen stores of one group of men by making them cycle for 2 minute bursts, over 90 minutes, the night before a test run of cycling at 50% of their maximum effort for 90 minutes. On another occasion the group was fed a high-carbohydrate diet the night before the test, with no exercise to reduce the fuel source.

Fat use in exercise was higher for the group which was carbohydrate depleted. The theory behind this is that fat will be used more as an energy source if there is little carbohydrate in the system. But while the theory appears to have worked in practice in the Dutch research, the potential dangers to the heart of this approach suggest it should never be used except under strict supervision, and usually only with people who are physically fit.

59.   Don't exercise to the point where you get out of breath

The body draws on two main sources for energy or fuel. The first of these, glucose or blood sugars, comes from carbohydrates in food. The second, fat, comes mainly from fat in the fat cells of the body which in turn comes from fat in food.

Glucose is the main type of fuel for vigorous intensive activity, whereas fat is used more in long duration, low-moderate intensity activity. As the activity moves from a sprint to a leisurely stroll, the body shifts from burning its limited supplies of glucose to burning its large supplies of fat.

Some fitness experts argue that because more total energy is used up at a high intensity, more fat will still be burned, even though the *proportion* of fat used as a fuel decreases. However, while this is true for fit people, it's much less likely to be true for fat people, who are usually less fit and burn less fat at a higher level of intensity than fit people.

The general principle therefore is that for optimal fat loss in most fat and unfit people, low-moderate intensity activity is best. If the activity is sufficiently intense to make you breathe too heavily or get out of breath, it's likely to be using up less fat as an energy source.

60. Don't dress too warmly when you exercise

For some time now, scientists have claimed that heat treatments for fat loss (in contrast to weight loss) don't work. If anything, they may increase weight by decreasing metabolic rate, or the rate at which the body burns energy to stay alive. In fact it may be the opposite, cold, which burns fat best.

Research by Canadian scientists with soldiers in the Arctic has shown that, even with a big increase in food intake, body fat is kept down by cold temperatures. The simple explanation for this is that the body uses up energy in the cold to maintain body heat.

You may think that the difference between a cold and a hot day is insignificant. But research carried out at New England University in New South Wales has shown that a temperature drop of even 5°C (i.e. from 28°C to 23°C) can lead to an average 10% increase in the body's metabolic rate in people wearing light clothes. This can amount to the equivalent of a large glass of beer in a day, or around about 5 kg of fat loss in a year.

So how realistic is the use of cold for fat loss?

While nobody is (yet) recommending freezers instead of sauna baths in gymnasiums for weight loss, there are indications that they might actually work better. In the meantime, some tips for the waist watcher might be:

- Avoid overheating by not overdressing in winter.
- Avoid excessively overheated buildings or vehicles.
- Wear clothes that allow the body to 'breathe', e.g. cottons rather than synthetics.
- Avoid heat treatments like saunas and steam baths.
- Exercise in the cooler part of the day (e.g. early mornings).

61.   Use a digital pedometer to measure your daily movement

Developments in digital pedometers, which give an indication of the amount of energy used up over the course of a day, have made these a useful addition to any weight loss or exercise program. Some new pedometers not only measure distance covered, but even estimate the calories used up during the effort. One version can even sense and measure forms of movement which don't involve movement over the ground, e.g. rowing or cycling.

The newer pedometers can be programmed to take into account the different stride lengths of such activities as walking up and down hills or between warming up and more extended jogging. Because they can be worn all day, the new pedometers give you a good indication of day-to-day variations in activity. If you're over or under your daily average, you can then compensate for this with other activities, or by cutting back on high energy foods.

62.   Change the type, intensity or frequency of exercise as you start to lose weight

The body adapts to the stressors placed on it. Exercise is a form of physical stressor, and physiological adaptation to any form of constant regular exercise will always eventually take place. This means that although you may continue to get health benefits and *maintain* a set body weight by carrying out a certain amount of exercise, you may no longer continue to *lose* weight or, more importantly, fat.

Making the body *less* efficient is going to use more energy.

Ironically, making the body *less* efficient is going to use more energy. So varying either the frequency, intensity, time or type of the exercise carried out is likely to be beneficial for fat loss once your body has become efficient at doing the exercise you've been doing.

63. Forget about swimming for weight loss

Swimming is usually one of the first exercises recommended for fitness or fatness. But while swimming may be fine (if used properly) for fitness and general all-round well-being, it's not an effective exercise for weight control. There are a number of reasons for this:

1. Because your body weight is supported in water, generally less overall energy is required to move at a set level of intensity in water.
2. Because fat floats, the fatter you are, the less energy you need to stay afloat and move in water.
3. The rate of energy expenditure in water is totally dependent on the level of efficiency of the swimmer. A very bad swimmer will burn more fat than a very good one.
4. Maintenance of core body temperature during and after swimming is much easier than maintaining it during or after land-based activities, thus energy is not used to return the body to its core temperature.

5. A lower centre of gravity and a greater proportion of body fat in females helps them float better than men and therefore use less energy in the water. Hence swimming is an even less effective exercise for fat loss in women than it's likely to be in men.

Swimming may be fine for fitness and general all-round well-being, but it's not an effective exercise for weight control.

None of the above negates the benefits of swimming, and particularly the more vigorous forms of aquarobics. The principal benefits, however, will be in fitness gains for high-intensity activity rather than in fatness loss, relative to other weight-bearing exercises such as walking.

64.   Aim to get the psychological rewards of exercise

For a de-conditioned person, any level of exercise can be discomfiting. However, with increased fitness, exercise can become its own reward. And while fitness is not necessarily a goal of an exercise program for weight loss, it will follow from even mild, regular exercise. There are three stages anyone may go through from being unfit to being fit:

Stage 1   The 'discomfort' stage is marked by getting out of breath easily, tiring quickly and not looking forward to any form of effort. It may last for days, weeks or even months. The type of motivation required to get through this stage is 'extrinsic' i.e. external to the individual.

Stage 2   The physical stage is marked by feelings of well-being *after* finishing exercising. The rewards are physical and tend to become more intrinsic as well as extrinsic. This means that the exercise itself begins to have a level of enjoyment leading to satisfaction.

Stage 3   The psychological stage: for many people, the third stage of fitness is when they begin to feel the psychological benefits which come with a high level of fitness. This is characterised by an enjoyment of the activity *while it's being carried out*. The rewards are totally intrinsic and the exercise becomes enjoyable in itself. Once you've got to this stage, it becomes much easier to maintain a lifetime exercise routine which in turn will help maintain a low body weight.

Although exercise is a vital part of any weight management program, it shouldn't be seen as the solution to all problems, as the effects of exercise on fat loss can be less than expected for various reasons.

There are many other benefits of exercise, however, including a feeling of well-being, better sleep, increased alertness and increased ability to function during the day. Improvements in these areas should be a primary goal of any exercise program. Losses in body fat should not be seen as the sole function of an exercise routine.

65.   Cool down slowly after exercise

During any form of physical activity the body's rate of energy use is increased. If the activity is carried out over an extended period at a low-moderate intensity, fat will be liberated from the fat cells to help fuel the body's extra energy needs.

Research on fat metabolism during and after exercise shows that the fats released from the fat cells remain in the bloodstream for some time, to be either oxidised in the muscles or returned to the fat cells if not utilised.

Cooling down quickly, through showering, for example, reduces the effort required by the body and hence reduces the amount of excess energy burned, while a gradual cool-down helps to maximise the exercise effort. It also decreases the risk of muscular injury occurring from not allowing circulating blood flow to re-supply tired muscles.

66. Do some moderate exercise before breakfast

Although time of day has not generally been considered important for influencing fat burning in exercise, some recent research has begun to question this. One study carried out at the University of Lausanne in Switzerland compared the amount of fat burned up as energy in exercising before and after breakfast. The researchers found that approximately 50% more fat is used up after an all night fast when exercise is carried out before eating (see figure below). They explained

THE PROPORTIONS OF FAT AND CARBOHYDRATE (CHO) USED AS ENERGY DURING EXERCISE BEFORE OR AFTER BREAKFAST
(from Schneiter et al, 1995)

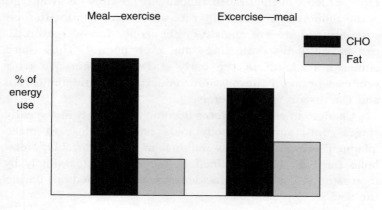

this as being due to the low levels of blood sugar available as a result of the 8–10 hours fast during sleep, with the result that the body calls on more fat to power the system.

Approximately 50% more fat is used up after an all night fast, when exercise is carried out before eating.

Any beneficial effect is overcome by eating immediately after exercise. The researchers found that the trick was not to eat for about 45 minutes after exercise.

67. If you're very fat, food restriction should come before exercise

When you gain weight, you put on lean body tissue (muscle) as well as fat, which is necessary to carry around the extra weight. Similarly, when you lose weight, around 25% of the weight lost is muscle and other lean body tissue.

For a very big person this may not be a disadvantage because it's often a loss in total body mass which is important—at least in the first instance. One possible disadvantage is the reduction in metabolic rate which may occur with food restriction alone. For many very big people, however, exercise can be quite discomforting—and even painful. Thus there comes a trade-off in the early stages of adherence to a program between the possible reductions in metabolic rate and the discomfort of exercise.

Changes in eating patterns become the priority in the early stages, until sufficient body mass has been lost to make 'planned' exercise, such as walking, more comfortable. Metabolic rate can be maintained in the early stages simply by increasing the amount of incidental activity carried out during the day.

68. Never (unless you're very fat) reduce food intake without exercising

Although we've recommended that diets should never be used, there's a role for overall food restriction, and particularly dietary fat restriction, in a fat loss program. Restriction of food energy, however, leads to a relatively indiscriminate loss of body tissue. It's estimated that up to 25% of the weight losses in an obese person can come from muscle, and the remaining 75% from fat. In a person who is not excessively overfat, the losses in muscle may be even higher, up to 50%.

Because muscle is more metabolically active than fat, muscle loss can lead to a reduction in metabolic rate which in turn can make it easier for the body to store fat at a later time. For the slightly overweight this can be a major disadvantage because they may end up being fatter than when they started. The problem becomes greater with greater energy restriction. More muscle will be lost on an 800 kcal/day diet than, for example, on a 1200 kcal/day diet.

Taking part in aerobic exercise can help maintain body muscle, however, even while fat is being lost. Because muscle tissue is being worked during aerobic exercise, the body is sufficiently discriminating not to cannibalise it as an energy source. Metabolism therefore remains high and fat loss (although not necessarily 'weight loss') is able to be maintained. For the overweight (in contrast to the obese) therefore, diets or food restriction should never be undertaken without a regular exercise program.

69. Start with incidental exercise only, if you're very fat

For a very big person, changes in eating patterns—particularly reductions in dietary fat intake—are the first priority in any weight loss program (see Tip 67). Planned exercise can even be counter-productive because the pain and effort may cause the individual to give up doing anything.

It's known that the bigger a person gets, the less likely he or she is to do the small movements that can help keep weight down. Instead of getting up to change the TV channel, for example, it's less uncomfortable to use the remote control. Small increases in this type of incidental exercise may be the only formal type of exercise added to the routine in the early stages.

As body weight begins to decrease and you begin to feel more active and energetic, a planned movement routine can be introduced to add to the benefit of changes in eating—but not until you're sure you can stick with it.

70. Use exercise when you are tempted to over-eat or are distressed

It's well known that one of the major stimulants to obesity is some form of stress. While acute stress generally leads to a decrease in eating, chronic stress, in the form of grief, anger, distress or depression, can lead to a reduction of inhibitions on over-eating and drinking and a reduction in physical activity. Over the long term this can lead to an alteration of energy balance and an increase in body fat.

The traditional responses to stress in evolution have been 'flight' or 'fight', both of which involve a significant degree of physical exertion. Exercise such as walking, if used as an alternative response to stress or the temptation to over-eat, can not only have a distraction effect, but may also help to reduce the physiological effects of the stress. In this way the stimulus–response connection between stress and over-eating may be broken.

71.   Wait a while after exercise before you eat

Athletes are generally recommended to replace the energy used during exercise by eating carbohydrate-rich foods immediately afterwards. While this practice is necessary to replace energy for fitness, it can have a counter-productive effect when exercise is being used to reduce body fatness (see Tip 66).

More fat is used as a result of an exercise session if you wait for 30–45 minutes after exercise before eating.

After exercise, circulating blood fats continue to be used as energy in the muscles to fuel the extra energy requirements of increased metabolism. If food is eaten immediately after exercise, particularly food high in carbohydrate which is quickly converted to blood glucose, the blood glucose will be used as the preferred source of energy. Circulating fats are then less likely to be metabolised and will be re-stored in the fat cells.

More fat will be used as a result of an exercise session if you wait 30–45 minutes after exercise before eating.

72.   Trade off walking for indulgences

A weight management program which is strict and inflexible is more likely to be abandoned at the first small transgression. For this reason, any program which you plan to maintain for a lifetime has to allow occasional indulgences.

There's a psychological process in accepting this philosophy. If you do allow yourself some transgressions, it's easier to accept them without feeling a failure. However, there's also a physiological process you can capitalise on. Indulgences usually involve the intake of too much energy, so you can compensate for them by an increase in energy output—that is, exercise.

The approximate energy value of a standard alcoholic drink is around 400 kJ. An average sized person uses about this amount of energy to walk 1 km. Trading off each drink with an extra kilometre of walking will help overcome the negative effects of the indulgence—and make life liveable.

Other common indulgences which can be traded off by doing extra walking or other exercise are eating chocolate, weekend breakfasts, business lunches, festive season over-imbibing and dinner at the inlaws.

73. Forget the callisthenics

Most 'fitness books' and articles on fitness in popular magazines have a section on callisthenics-type exercises. These, we're told, will lead to increased fitness and muscular strength and even, if you're lucky, the body you've always desired.

The main function of exercise in a weight management program is to burn energy—preferably fat. Because of their limited duration and specific muscle orientation, callisthenic exercises have little value in fat burning compared to extended duration aerobic activities such as walking or cycling. It's a bit like the difference between the petrol used up in taking your car for a long drive compared to revving it up a few times on the spot.

Callisthenics may be good for toning up muscles. But concentrate on getting rid of the fat so you can see your muscles before you even think about trying to tone them up!

74.   Forget the sit-ups: go for a walk instead

Because men usually store fat around the waist and because sit-ups work the abdominal muscles, it's often assumed that the best cure for a pot belly is thousands of sit-ups. The pot belly, however, consists mainly of fat overlying a small band of abdominal muscle. Fat is metabolised through long, continuous, general aerobic activity, whereas sit-ups work a specific muscle group.

**Sit-ups only serve to give
you a 'tight fat belly'
rather than a
'loose fat belly'.**

Because underlying muscle is toned up through sit-ups, sit-ups in the absence of a general aerobic program only serve to give you a 'tight fat belly' rather than a 'loose fat belly'. The fat is likely to remain—on top of the muscle.

75.   Ignore exercises for spot reduction

Many people think that to reduce fat from a certain part of the body all you need to do is exercise that part of the body. If this were true gum chewers would all have skinny faces!

Fat is stored in fat cells all over the body. Fat is taken from these cells as a fuel source for muscles in an order determined by gender, genetics and a range of other factors. As a general rule, it comes off the last place it's gone on. So if you've porked up recently around the middle, the first place the extra fat will come off—even in response to an exercise that doesn't use the abdominal muscles, such as walking—will be the waist.

Specific exercises for the gluteal muscles, often promoted to reduce fat on women's buttocks, may even have a counter-productive effect. Lower body fat in women is known to be resistant to the normal stimuli causing a breakdown of fat, probably because of the evolutionary need for such fat as an energy reserve in pregnancy. Exercises for the gluteals thus may increase the size of the gluteal muscles but not result in any fat loss—at least not from that part of the body.

76. If walking is a problem, try a weight-supportive exercise

We've said it many times—walking is one of the best forms of exercise around for weight control. However, because it's a weight-bearing exercise (i.e. the body's own weight is carried), walking may not be suitable for everyone, such as people with lower limb injuries. In these cases, walking can be substituted by a weight-supportive exercise such as cycling, swimming, aquarobics or rowing.

Including swimming may appear to be a paradox, because we eliminated it in Tip 63 as an efficient form of fat-loss exercise. But where other forms of weight-bearing activity are unsuitable, swimming may be the best option available. Aquarobics, or exercises in water, provide an even better option as they can use large amounts of energy with little discomfort.

77. To slim children down, decrease their inactivity rather than increase their activity

Almost one in three children in Australia under the age of 18 are now regarded as overfat or obese. Much of this is put down to inactivity, in particular to competing behaviours which decrease physical activity in children, e.g. watching TV, playing video games.

The effect of excessive hours in front of a TV set concerns many experts in obesity. Decreasing time in front of the TV, however, may be more important, and easier, than trying to get fat kids involved in physical activities which they don't like. This was put to the test by scientists at Pittsburgh University, who compared a program to reward obese 8–12 year olds for decreasing inactive behaviours with

RECOMMENDATIONS FOR EXERCISE FOR HEALTH AND WEIGHT CONTROL

DO LEAST
Watching TV
Sitting around
Playing computer games

DO MOST DAYS
Put together at least 30 minutes of
one or more mild to moderate forms of
exercise: walking, dancing, swimming,
gym activities, aerobics, bike riding, gardening,
jogging or sports. This can be done in one session
or in separate sessions of e.g. 10 minutes each.

DO AS OFTEN AS POSSIBLE
Choose the more active option in day-to-day activities. For
example take the stairs, park further away from your destination,
reduce use of remote controls and other labour-saving devices,
walk or cycle instead of driving, walk to a further bus or train stop...

INCREASE TOTAL MOVEMENT

another program designed to increase their involvement in sport and physical activity.

The researchers found greater decreases in the percentage overweight in the decreased sedentary group than in the increased active group, or in a combined group which was encouraged to both decrease sedentary activity and increase exercise.

Techniques to decrease sedentary behaviour included the use of daily log books by the children being studied, and the development of contracts by the children with their parents. If sedentary activity decreased to a pre-set agreed level, parents would reward the child with a pre-agreed reward.

For a fat child, therefore, turning the television or the computer off may be a more effective technique for weight loss than trying to get that child involved in a sport or other active pastime.

78.   Now, put it all together

As we've seen, exercise for fat loss can be quite different to exercise for fitness. We've looked at the importance of incidental and planned exercise. We've also looked at different types of exercises. But, just so you don't get confused, we've put together the recommendations for exercise for fat loss in a pyramid style, modelled after some work on exercise for health. Check the pyramid and see whether it fits in with what you're doing—or more importantly, what you plan to do.

3

MAINTAINING YOUR LOSSES

Anyone can lose *weight*. It's losing *fat* that's the problem. Even so, it's not that difficult to *lose* fat if you know a little bit about food and exercise. But keeping it off—that's a different story.

The reported long-term success rate for most weight control programs is somewhere between 5% and 20%. That is, only 5%–20% of those ever attempting to take weight off are successful in keeping it off for up to two years. (In scientific circles any measurement period less than two years is not regarded as serious.)

The problem is that the human body was designed to gain and lose fat as external conditions dictate. Unfortunately, at least in this day and age, it's much easier to gain than to lose. This was important from an evolutionary perspective because gains in fat in the good times meant greater survival in the bad. If, on the other hand, losses came easily, humans wouldn't have survived the lean times throughout history to get us to today's Western situation of plenty.

To resist fat losses, the body adapts by reducing the rate

71

of energy which it burns at rest (the metabolic rate) and during activity, and increasing the appetite. Where food is available (as in the modern supermarket society), these changes in body function can be just a little too hard to resist. So back go those precious kilos you've fought so hard to keep off—unless . . . by understanding the principles of adaptation you can turn those principles to your own advantage.

79.   Learn the techniques for maintaining weight loss

According to Dr Tim Wadden, a psychologist from the University of Pennsylvania, the clues to the successful maintenance of fat loss come from studying the habits of those who are successful over the long term. This suggests that:

- Although diet may be important in helping to lose weight, those who develop a lifetime pattern of exercise manage to keep it off better.
- Greater maintenance occurs in women who do long, regular (although not necessarily vigorous) exercise like walking.
- People who regularly eat just one fatty food have no increased risk of regaining weight. But those who eat two might just as well eat six—all are a recipe for relapse.
- Most successful weight-loss maintainers:
  - don't count calories, but develop a personal eating plan
  - exercise regularly
  - closely monitor their weight
  - monitor their food intake.
- Best maintenance comes from setting realistic goals. In some severely obese people there may be biological limits to big reductions. Satisfaction with more modest goals can improve the situation.

Other research has shown that the best long-term maintainers are those who also have a well-developed means of dealing with stress. This prevents any relapse into over-eating or under-exercising following periods of psychological upheaval.

80. Recognise the greater difficulty in maintaining fat loss if you've previously been obese

According to Danish scientists, people who have lost large amounts of weight have more trouble keeping it off than lean people have staying lean. This may be partly because there are differences in the rate at which formerly fat people and lean people burn food as energy after a meal. If a meal is high in fat, the formerly obese tend to store the fat more readily in the fat cells of their body, and rely more on blood sugars from carbohydrate as their energy source.

People who have lost large amounts of weight have more trouble keeping it off than lean people have staying lean.

Due to the body's limited ability to store blood sugars from carbohydrate (only about 450 g or 2100 kcals in total), the greater carbohydrate usage in formerly fat people leads to a more rapid depletion of these blood sugars. Low blood sugar signals hunger to the brain, and thus increases the likelihood of subsequent food intake.

The implications of this are that someone who has previously been obese, but who has lost a lot of weight, needs to take great care with diet. Losing fat is only half the problem. Keeping it off is the main game.

81. Set short-term 'process' goals

Most people have a long-term goal in mind when they take on a weight control program. But relying on your long-term goal alone can be self-defeating, as it can take such a long time to get there and progress will be interrupted by plateaus along the way. It's advisable therefore to have short-term *process* goals, as well as the long-term *outcome* goal, which can be used as marker points along the way. You can set these over one week, one month or one year, but they should be clearly defined.

A process goal means achieving something in the process of reaching your outcome goal. If a process goal is reached, there's at least some encouragement to continue. Process goals can include cutting fat back to 40 grams a day, walking 6 days a week, walking a set distance each day, reducing total food intake, not eating a particular fatty food, increasing daily energy expenditure, cutting back on margarine or butter etc.

82. Accept gradual weight losses

Fluctuations in body weight are accompanied by physiological adaptations designed to return the body to the status quo. In particular, a sudden decrease in body mass will lead to a decrease in metabolic rate and an increase in appetite.

Decreases of over 1.5 kg per week have been shown to be associated with an increased risk of gallstones and a range of other possible health problems.

Large, sudden changes can be expected to result in large physiological adaptations, which may ultimately have a counter-productive effect on long-term fat losses. Gradual losses on the other hand allow the body to adjust to changes with less negative impact.

Medical research has also shown some health risks associated with large, sudden losses. Decreases of over 1.5 kg per week have been shown to be associated with an increased risk of gallstones, for example, and a range of other possible problems. The recommended safe rate of loss is between 0.5–1 kg per week. If a waist measurement is used as the outcome goal (as it should be, particularly for men), about a 1% loss per week is recommended on acceptable programs such as GutBusters.

83.   Don't do anything you can't maintain for a lifetime

Long-term weight loss means making changes that are liveable. It's not feasible to expect to stay on a diet of self-denial for life. This is why diets don't work. Nor can one expect, for example, that a middle aged man will suddenly stop drinking alcohol and stay off it for the rest of his life. More to the point, once one element of self-denial is abandoned, the greater the prospect of the whole program being abandoned.

It's not feasible to expect to stay on a diet of self-denial for life. This is why diets don't work.

Realistically, any changes that are made to reduce body fat and maintain a long-term weight loss must be changes that can be made for life. And while some changes may take a while to adapt to (for example, it can take from two weeks to six months to get used to eating low-fat meals), most will improve your feeling of well-being and make you want to keep doing them. The moral is, if you can't imagine yourself doing it for life, do something else.

84. Appreciate that if you're not gaining, you're winning

Any loss of weight is accompanied by adjustments which make further losses more difficult. In a sense, the body fights against a movement away from an equilibrium level of body fat to which it has become accustomed. It does this in three main ways:

1. *There is a decrease in metabolic rate*: As about 70% of the body's daily energy expenditure comes from metabolism, even a small change in metabolic rate can lead to a large impact on body fat stores. Research shows that adjustments to metabolic rate actually exceed decreases in body mass, i.e. a 10% loss in weight may lead to a 20% reduction in metabolic rate, thus tending to slow, and perhaps even reverse, the decline in weight.

2. *There are changes in body composition*: Not all of the weight which is lost in a typical weight loss program comes from fat. In the average overweight person, about 25% of weight loss comes from muscle. Because muscle is more metabolically active than fat, this means a decline in the overall rate of energy use which in turn slows down the process of fat loss.

3. *There are increases in hunger and appetite*: Reductions in body weight are usually balanced centrally (in the brain) by increases in appetite which reduce the long-term effectiveness of the fight against fat loss. In many cases these increases in appetite are so subtle that they're not noticed. But the outcome in terms of energy intake are certainly recognised by the body.

Natural decreases in body weight don't happen in a linear fashion, but in a series of plateaus, as shown in the graph

ACTUAL AND THEORETICAL TRENDS
IN WEIGHT LOSS

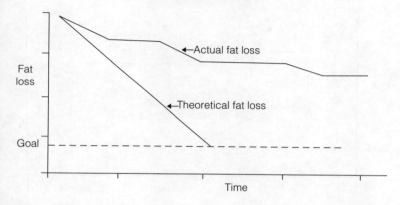

above. The length of the plateau and the size of the drop-off is probably dependent on the length of time the body has been at that particular level. The main thing is recognising that being on a plateau means you're still winning! Only when you start gaining again do you start losing the battle.

85.   To break through a plateau, change

Plateaus in fat loss come about largely as a result of the body adapting to a different level of energy balance, either in the form of reduced energy input or increased energy output. Theoretically at least, there may be a breakthrough in a fat-loss plateau by decreasing the body's ability to adapt. This would result through changing something. In relation to exercise, this could be:

1. *Intensity*: increase the speed at which your exercise is carried out.
2. *Duration*: exercise for longer periods if possible.
3. *Frequency*: exercise more regularly (e.g. by adding 'incidental' exercise during the day).

FAT LOSS IN THE LONG-TERM AND SHORT-TERM OVERWEIGHT

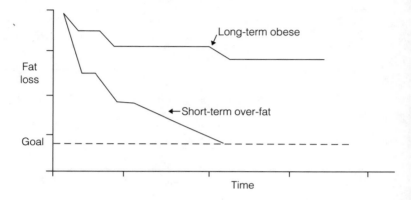

4. *Type*: vary walking with cycling, swimming, aerobics—
anything you like doing.

With food intake as the other side of the energy equation,
you can help break through plateaus by:

1. *Decreasing calorie intake*: but only where this is still high.
2. *Increasing calorie intake*: by re-feeding (i.e. slowly
   increasing the amount of food eaten) where the calorie
   intake has been too low (i.e. under 1000 kcals/day) and
   has been so for long periods.
3. *Decreasing fat intake more*: to lower the appetite as well
   as calories.
4. *Changing the food type*: eating foods the body is not
   familiar with or which you haven't had for a long time
   (but are still low in fat).

The body adjusts physiologically to changes in body mass
by changing metabolism, hunger and the rate at which
energy is burned for a given amount of exercise. If overweight or obesity has been a persistent problem, these
physiological adjustments become more rigid. It's as if the

body is saying to itself: 'I'm fine at this weight—at least I'm alive—so I'll fight to stay there.'

Fat losses are therefore likely to be smaller and plateaus, where no weight is lost, are likely to be longer depending on the duration of obesity. This is shown in the graph opposite. Anecdotally, we would have to say that this is not always the case. But if you've been fat for a long time, you can't expect to get skinny overnight.

86. If at first you don't succeed, persist

The longer you've carried extra weight, the harder your body is likely to fight to stay that way. And while plateauing is an inevitable process of any weight loss, it's likely to be even more important for the long-term obese. In some cases the body can resist a weight change for months—even in the presence of large changes in energy balance.

Where this is the case, you may notice other metabolic improvements; you may feel fitter, be sleeping better, even *feel* a little lighter, although you may actually *be* heavier (because of an increase in the ratio of muscle to fat due to exercise). The body can't resist forever, however. Ultimately it will need to adjust to the fact that the new energy balance is now the new status quo. This will only happen through persistence.

If you're confident that you've made the proper changes (i.e. you're not kidding yourself about the amount of food you're eating or the exercise you're doing), persistence will eventually pay off. It may not happen overnight, but it will happen.

87. Redefine success

Short-term losses in weight shouldn't be thought of as the only measure of success in a weight control program. Short-term rapid weight loss is usually short-lived, and hence only success over a two year period or longer is regarded seriously.

More importantly, it has now been shown that improve-

WHY FISHERMEN ARE FAT.

ments in health and disease risk can occur on a weight control program without any apparent loss in weight. These improvements are usually accompanied by feelings of well-being, improvements in self-esteem and even some changes in body composition (i.e. fat loss combined with muscle gain).

Success therefore needs to be redefined to include such obvious things as:

- Decreases in medication
- Improved quality of life and feelings of well-being
- Increased physical activity
- Reduced fat intake
- Better digestion
- Better sleep patterns
- Greater feelings of energy during the day
- Less tiredness

Where these changes are used as signals of success, less concern will be placed on actual weight loss. This can often lead to the paradoxical effect of greater weight loss over the long term.

88.   Learn how to manage stress

Long-term chronic stress has an effect on body fat levels because it can:

- *Encourage nervous over-eating*: In some people stress decreases the appetite, but in others it makes them pig out to the max. It's not just to do with those nervous hands. Food provides a kind of comfort—it feels good—when all about you might feel bad.

- *Increase alcohol consumption*: Alcohol is a great way to blot out the effects of stress. Whatever you'd like to do to solve your problems, in your fantasies you can do it after a few drinks. The trouble is, it doesn't last. Alcohol is a short-term solution to stress but a long-term solution to a flat stomach.

- *Immobilise*: Not wanting to move is a symptom of severe or chronic stress. Not moving means not burning up energy. Not burning up energy means getting fat. Animals put in continued stressful situations from which they can't escape actually give up and become totally immobilised. This syndrome is called 'learned helplessness' by psychologists. A similar thing can happen to people.

- *Decrease feelings of self control*: The loss of *control* over one's life is one of the main symptoms (and causes) of stress. If this flows through to other aspects of life, control over weight loss and health practices will also occur.

- *Increase mobilisation of fatty acids*: One of the (apparent) benefits of stress in fat loss is that it mobilises fats from fat stores to be used as energy. However, if there's no accompanying movement or exercise to use up this fat, it will remain in the bloodstream and can tend to clog arteries and cause heart problems. This is one of the main health ill-effects of stress.

- *Decrease self-esteem*: For many individuals, an increase in stress leads to a reduction in self-esteem which then flows through to all other aspects of life (including fat control).

Coping with stress is an important component of long-term weight management. Thus stress management is often a proxy way of facilitating long-term weight loss.

89.   Don't worry about small changes of weight during festive seasons

One of the biggest dangers for anyone on a weight reduction program is the festive season. Temptations abound—parties, dinners, drinks—with not much time for physically working it off.

A typical advance is retreat. You know you're not going to win at this time so you may as well fatten up and enjoy it. The trouble is, there comes a payback time—and bills always seem to come around quicker than income!

If your adult body weight is 8–10 kg more than your body weight at age 20, it might be time to start to do something about it.

A more realistic approach is the 'passive pause'. Don't worry about not continuing to lose. As long as you're not gaining, you're in front. You can also get back on the wagon when things die down. And it's not nearly as hard to climb back on the wagon if you haven't fallen hard on your head.

English obesity expert Dr John Garrow has shown that small gains and losses in body weight during the course of a lifetime have no apparent ill-effects on health. If your adult body weight is more than around 8–10 kg than your body weight at age 20, on the other hand, it might be time to start to do something about it.

90. Be careful of 'weight cycling'

Researchers at UCLA in California claim that although being fat is unhealthy, 'weight cycling', moving constantly from fat to thin, has even greater health risks.

'Most studies done on weight variability show that the greater the number and size of weight changes, the greater the risk,' says Dr Judith Stern, from UCLA's Davis campus.

One possible reason for this is that in the weight-loss phase, muscle is lost as well as fat. When weight is regained, it's regained just in the form of fat, which can be in the dangerous intra-abdominal area.

Research from the University of Minnesota also indicates that the bigger the weight gain from age 20 to later adulthood, the greater the risk of suffering or dying from a weight-related disease—diabetes, heart disease, stroke, cancer, etc. 'Weight gains of 20 lb [9 kg] increase the risk dramatically,' says Dr Robert Jeffries. Although it's probably not so bad, and even natural, to put on some more fat in later life, too much gain can become too much of a burden.

Stability, it seems, is the name of the game. And preferably stability at the weight around age 20.

HEALTH PROBLEMS OF TOO RAPID WEIGHT LOSS

- Gall bladder disease
- Altered sleep
- Anaemia
- Constipation
- Irregular menstruation
- Eating disorders

---

91. Don't weigh, measure

There has long been controversy about the best measure of body fat to use in a weight-loss program. Weight doesn't necessarily reflect fat (although it's generally a good indication). More accurate measures of body fat are usually too complicated or too expensive for use by other than elite athletes.

Researchers at the University of Glasgow, however, have shown that a simple measurement around the waist is as good as other more complicated techniques.

The researchers, in the University's Department of Human Nutrition, compared waist-to-hip ratio measurements and body mass index (a measure of weight divided by height squared) to get cut-off points for recommendations for the general public.

**Bathroom scales are not
only unnecessary, but
downright undesirable.**

Measuring around the waist, midway between the iliac crest (top of the hip-bone) and the lower rib, they found that:

- Men with a waist circumference of more than 102 cm and women more than 88 cm have an increased health risk and should reduce their body fat.
- Men with a waist circumference of 94–102 cm and women between 80–88 cm should be cautioned not to get any fatter if they want to stay healthy.

The easy to remember figures of 100 cm for men and 90 cm for women are regarded as functional cut-off points—irrespective of height—which indicate a threshold level for health risk. Waist measurements can also be used (particularly in men) as a good indication of progress in a fat-loss program.

92. Don't get too excited by your BMI measurement

The most frequently used simple measure of fatness has been body mass index (BMI), a measure of weight (in kilograms) divided by height (in metres) squared. BMI scores of between 19–25 are regarded as 'normal'.

BMI has tended to provide a reasonable indication of population levels of excess body fatness. However, the use of weight in the equation makes it much less valid as a measure for individuals, or as a measure of change in body fat. Athletic men, in particular, are discriminated against because of a high muscle mass which also tends to be heavy. Body stature can also influence BMI measures in some females.

One recent comparison of BMI with a 'gold standard' measure of body fatness (i.e. duel energy X-ray absorptiometry, or DXA), has shown that less than two-thirds of the variance in percentage fat in adults is predicted by BMI, and this is even lower in adolescents. In females, a BMI of 20 kg/m^2 can correspond to a body fat percentage ranging from 13–32%. Without any change in BMI, there can also be a change in body fat % of + or – 5%. Hence the use of BMI as a measure of body fat, or change in body fat, is suspect, to say the least.

93. Try to have at least two alcohol-free days a week

Alcohol *per se* is not thought to be fattening (see Tip 38). However, alcohol consumed in conjunction with fat in the diet (or even a very high intake of carbohydrate) may save the fat (which might otherwise be used immediately as energy) to be kept in the fat stores.

Alcohol also reduces inhibition, so that it's harder to refuse fatty foods after a drink. For this reason 1 or 2 alcohol-free days a week may help reduce the potential for fat storage. AFDs also appear to have a health benefit, although the reasons for this are not known. The easiest days for most people to reduce alcohol intake are usually early in the week (Monday–Wednesday).

94.   Extend your week till Friday night

Market research surveys have shown that people eat less fats and sugars, drink less alcohol, eat breakfast more often and generally behave in ways more conducive to maintaining their health earlier in the week. There is a slight dip in their resolve by about Wednesday (as is is well known to any restaurant or nightclub owner), with a gradual decline to the 'Friday night swill'. Saturday is usually a write-off and the whole cycle begins again on Sunday night.

Extending the week till Friday night allows more opportunity to trade off the weekend's lapses in behaviour. This way you can allow yourself some indulgences (as if you've earned them) without accompanying guilt.

95.   Watch your inhibitions after a drink

The scientific literature on the fattening effects of alcohol is quite convincing; alcohol *per se* does not appear to directly increase the laying down of body fat. However, there is a danger in taking this too literally because there are other factors associated with alcohol use that may mitigate against leaness.

In the first place, alcohol decreases your inhibitions. This is one of the main reasons many people drink; it helps them to relax and be more themselves—*in vino veritas*, as they say. But the release of inhibitions can also release the inhibition to gorge on foods that are fattening. While it may be possible to resist that tempting morsel when stone cold sober, the temptation is more inviting under the cloud of inhibitory release. Unless you're convinced of your moral fortitude under such circumstances, it may be wise to go lightly on the mental relaxant.

96.   Beware of the effects of critical times

During certain times of your life it's easy for things like maintaining a steady body weight to go wrong. Forewarned is forearmed, so awareness of the following critical periods may be crucial:

- *Marriage*: Marriage, or its equivalent, often leads to both partners tending to gain fat and decrease fitness. Research carried out at Sydney University shows that this is particularly so for young men, possibly due to a decreased level of physical activity through less involvement in organised sport, and increased regular food intake.

- *Retirement from sport*: Keeping up the high food intake necessary to fuel the increased energy level for sport can become a habit. Retirement from sporting activity often takes place suddenly; the drastic decrease in energy usage combines with the habit of a high energy intake and leads to increases, or rebounds, in fatness.

- *Changing a job*: Changes in the work environment can disrupt your downward body fat momentum. It's not clear why this should be so, but obviously changes in attitude and perhaps the desire to impress could have an impact.

- *Middle age in males*: Decreases in metabolic rate, which occur around the rate of 2% per decade from age 20, start to have a significant impact on males around 40–50 years of age. Couple this with the stresses of mid-life and other problems that occur around this time and you've got a ready-made fat rebound. Be ready for it.

- *Grief and bereavement*: Bereavement is a period of chronic stress where fat control become less important than surviving. Exercise decreases and food intake, particularly of comfort foods, increases. Depending on circumstances, this can last for anything from a couple of months to a couple of years. Dealing with the loss is the most important thing at this time, but try to at least to stay on a plateau.

- *Divorce or separation*: Like bereavement, divorce or separation has the potential for great psychological disruption. Again, the primary concern is to deal with the psychological problems associated with the event. Try not to put it on, and get through the problem. Moving house, particularly to another city, with the accompanying breakdown of support networks, has the same result.

- *Periods of prolonged stress*: Stress reduces the effectiveness of barriers to restraint. (In some cases, particularly of acute stress, food intake is actually reduced and fat can be lost.) In chronic, non-life-threatening stress, the opposite can occur, however, and can be accompanied by an increase in drinking to cope with the stress. Learn to recognise upcoming stress periods and to deal with them so they don't interfere with weight loss, because getting fat again will only increase your stress level!

- *After quitting smoking*: It's well known that smokers who quit will gain an average of around 3.5 kg of body weight over 12 months. This is largely due to the reversal of the effects of nicotine (which elevates the basal metabolic rate) and the reduced food intake associated with smoking (possibly because a smoker's hands are always busy). Still, it's more healthy to be a fat non-smoker than a lean smoker. The fat-gaining effects do pass after a while.

- *A side effect of some prescribed medications*: A number of medications, including those prescribed for anxiety, depression, schizophrenia and tissue repair (e.g. cortisol), can increase body fat. Check with your doctor if you suspect such an effect and ask for an alternative drug if it's available.

- *During festive periods*: For most people, festive periods—including Christmas, Easter, birthdays, reunions and other cultural and individual celebrations—are a time when enjoyment overrules austerity. After all, life is for living.

The main rule is to make sure you don't go up again—
even if there are no losses! If maintenance can ensure
stability, it becomes more feasible, both psychologically
and physiologically, to continue with improvements at a
later time.

97.   Eat less and/or move more as you get older

Energy expenditure declines naturally with age, largely as a
result of decreases in muscle mass of around 1 kg per
decade. Metabolic rate declines with muscle mass, at the
rate of about 2% per decade, meaning that if you eat and
drink and exercise the same as you did when you were young,
you're guaranteed to put on extra poundage naturally.

**The natural slowdown in
energy use and growth
requirements as you get
older, means that just to
keep your weight stable
you have to take in less
food and/or do a little
more exercise as the
years progress.**

Contrary to popular belief, more attention needs to be
given to maintaining energy output or modifying energy
input with age to ensure body fat doesn't balloon out. The
natural slowdown in energy use and growth requirements as
you get older means that just to keep your weight stable
you either have to take in *less* food and/or exercise a little
more as the years progress. As it's usually a little difficult
to compete with your youth on the exercise side, you generally have to be more careful on the food intake side.

There's one happy message from this. Research with animals, as well as with humans, shows that those who eat less tend to live longer and remain healthier. (But isn't it a cruel twist of fate, that things don't get easier just when you feel they ought to?)

98. *Reduce* your efficiency

As explained earlier, maintenance of weight loss beyond a certain point is not only unlikely, it's downright unhealthy. Your body adapts, to stop you disappearing. And the way it does this is by becoming *more efficient* at what you've given it to do.

Walking 3–4 kilometres a day at the start of a program may be a bit of a shock to most people's systems. But after even a week or two, those muscles involved in walking spring back to life and do it quite easily. Where it took, for example, around 400 kJ to walk 1 km in 12 minutes at the start, it may now take only 360 kJ.

Because you've lost a couple of kilos of fat, your body also has to work less hard to keep you alive (your metabolic rate). Both of these things mean you've become more efficient, using less energy—and less fat. Strangely enough, you need to become *less* efficient again to burn *more* energy. Walking on your hands would do it, but that's not always feasible (or advisable). But certainly changing the type, duration or intensity of the exercise is. Even changing the path you normally take for a walk, or the time of day you do it, may help.

The same applies to the type of food you eat. It takes energy to digest food (more to digest carbohydrate than fat) and any change in eating patterns can increase total energy (and fat) loss. You need to become a *less efficient* eater if you want to get off a fat-loss plateau. You can do this by trying different foods—fruits and vegetables in season for example, or something you rarely eat, like Mongolian or Tyrolean fare. Even—and this is a long shot—try a different drink, gin and tonic instead of a beer, and see if it helps.

If you've hit a fat-loss plateau, or are about to, becoming *less* efficient could be just what the fat doctor ordered—even if it's not what the productivity consultant desires.

99. If you only have a bit of fat to lose, don't just restrict your food intake

Weight loss consists inevitably of muscle as well as fat. The proportion of muscle to fat lost decreases proportionally with increases in the fat to muscle ratio. The amount of muscle lost is also dependent on the mode of energy balance—if muscle is used through physical activity, it's less likely to be metabolised for fuel than if the mode of weight loss is food restriction alone.

**Food restriction alone
becomes more
counter-productive to fat
loss the less body fat there
is to lose—a point which
is lost on many dieting
young women trying for
that extra 'anorexic
model' look.**

Muscle loss, in turn, can be counter-productive to a fat-loss program because it will result in a decrease in metabolism and hence increase the potential for a greater gain in body fat at some later stage.

A relatively lean person with only a small amount of fat to lose would lose a greater proportion of muscle to fat following a food restriction program than a person with a greater proportion of body fat. Food restriction alone becomes more counter-productive to fat loss the less body fat there is to lose—a point which is lost on many dieting young women trying for that extra 'anorexic model' look.

100. Beware the change of seasons

Seasonal affective disorder (SAD) is a phenomenon found in a small group of weight-sensitive people. The disorder is characterised by large gains in weight in the winter, often 'balanced' by losses instigated by purging and severe food restriction in summer.

SAD is usually more common in countries with greater differences between the seasons than in Australia. It's thought to have a physiological cause through lack of daylight, possibly affecting a chemical called melatonin, which is involved in skin tanning and body biorhythms. (Melatonin has recently been prescribed for the prevention of jet lag in long distance travellers). Research is now also examining the effects of artificial light on reducting SAD.

Although a reasonably rare phenomenon, a minor form of SAD may occur in some people who tend to over-eat and under-exercise in the winter months. Awareness of the effects of the change in seasons may help overcome this— but we can't guarantee it.

4

THE INFLUENCE OF THE ENVIRONMENT

The emphasis on molecular research in the field of obesity in recent years has taken our attention away from the real causes of obesity. It's undoubtedly true that there are genes that make getting fat easy and getting thinner difficult for some people. But if genetics are the only cause of the problem, why hasn't a large proportion of the human population been as fat for thousands of years as it is now?

The answer lies in the interaction between genes and the environment. Changes in the gene pool don't occur in a short time span—in one, two, or even ten generations. They take hundreds, and in some cases thousands, of years. This suggests the genes for obesity have been around for a long time. We need therefore to look at the environment in which obesity exists to see what's changed to allow the genetic causes of obesity to become manifest.

You don't need to be Einstein to work out the answer. In Western industrialised countries, high energy, dense, (fatty) foods have become abundant through modern techniques of food manufacturing and marketing, at the same time as machines and technology have made daily movement almost a thing of the past. Put the two together and you have a wonderful opportunity for the genes which make the excess body fat which was so important for survival in earlier times to go wild.

The tips in this chapter cover changing your environment. They may also help you reduce any guilt you may feel at not being as successful at losing weight as you expected.

101. Accept the fact that weight management in an industrialised environment is not easy

Modern medicine has solved all sorts of problems—infections, genetic disorders, environmental diseases. So why can't it cure the fastest growing problem in Western societies—obesity?

According to Spanish obesity expert Professor Xavier Formiguera, there are four main reasons:

MIDAS FORMICA TAKES ON THE WORLD ARMED ONLY WITH A LUNCHBOX AND A WATER BOTTLE.

1. Obesity has a multifactorial origin: There's no one single cause of obesity. For some people, wrong eating is the problem, for others, too little movement; for others again, there's a psychological component. To deal with multiple causes requires multiple solutions—and these are rarely available.

2. The nature of the disorder makes it mandatory that it is treated for life: 'Weight loss' is easy. 'Long-term fat loss' is hard. To maintain fat loss over an extended period is the hardest of all, and requires a lifetime commitment to a treatment which is often not acceptable. The implication is that if something is going to work, it has to be able to be maintained for a lifetime.

3. The treatment is more painful than the disease: Obesity or overweight, for most people, is painless. They've lived with it for many years and have suffered little more than its psychological disadvantages. The potential treatment on the other hand is restrictive—reduced capacity to eat, drink and be merry! Unlike infections and other diseases, who wouldn't prefer the disease to the cure?

4. Just as there are many causes of obesity, there may be many treatments: Many people carrying excess flab may be unable to deal with the problem on their own, and may need the help of a range of disciplines—medicine, psychology, psychiatry, exercise. The diversity of the problem points to the need for a diversity of treatments, which currently doesn't seem to exist—at least not in the one place.

A fifth reason we could add to this list is the modern environment. Human beings have always had the potential to get fat but their historical environment has tended to act against it. Today's modern industrialised environment provides ready access to high energy-dense foods with little need to use up energy to acquire them. If a stable body weight is to be maintained in a modern society, the environment needs to be controlled.

102. Learn label lingo

The 1990s supermarket contains thousands of foods with an assortment of nutritional claims which can leave even the keenest shopper bewildered. A *Choice* magazine survey of 408 shoppers in New South Wales, for example, found that many people were not aware of the true meaning of the common nutritional claims. Here's a summary of what the survey revealed:

- *'Reduced'*, *'lower'*, *'less'*—More than 50% regarded these terms as absolute, meaning, for example, that reduced-fat cheese has the same fat content as 'reduced-fat' yoghurt. People confused these terms with 'low-fat'.
- *'Light' and 'lite'*—Over half thought yoghurts labelled 'light' or 'lite' had a lower or low-fat content than yoghurts not so labelled—and they were right. But 33% also believed that oils so labelled were low or lower in fat than other oils (when the labels actually referred to the colour of the oil).
- *'% fat-free'*—Some thought that a 97% fat-free frozen dessert was completely fat-free. Others thought that a 90% fat-free mayonnaise was low in fat (but not when they realised it contained 10% fat). Almost half surveyed thought that 80% fat-free mince was lower in fat than lean mince—incorrect.
- *'Fights cholesterol' and 'cholesterol free'*—Almost one-third thought that the 'fights cholesterol' claim on a margarine meant lower or low food cholesterol—and they were correct. However, one in ten thought the tag also meant the margarine was low in fat or fat-free.
- *'No added sugar'*—About half thought products labelled 'no added sugar' contained little or no sugar. But these claims are most often found on products fairly high in natural sugars, like fruit juice and jam.

The Australian National Food Authority (NFA) has pro-

Nutritional claims about fat and what they mean

WHAT IT SAYS	WHAT IT MEANS
Reduced fat Lower fat Less fat	The food must not contain more than 75% of the total fat content of the same quantity of the regular item.
Low fat Low in fat	Not more than 3 g total fat per 100 g of food or 1.5 g total fat per liquid food. If the claim is made for a food naturally or intrinsically low in fat, it must refer to the whole class of similar foods. For example, a 'low-fat' claim for pasta must note that 'pasta is a low-fat food'.
Fat free	No more than 0.15 g of fat per 100 g of food.
% fat free	The food must meet the requirements for 'low fat' and must carry a statement of the actual fat content (expressed as a percentage of the food) close to the claim.
% free	Cannot be used to refer to any other nutrient other than fat.
Lite or light	The characteristic which makes the food light must be stated on the label. The term may not necessarily apply to fat content, but also to colour or flavour.
Diet	This claim most often applies to foods which have an energy content significantly lower than that at which a 'reduced energy' claim can be made. Unless other criteria are met the food must: (a) have an energy content not more than 60% of the reference food; (b) have a reduced energy content of at least 170 kJ per 100 g of food (80 kJ per 100 g of liquid food); and (c) carry a statement of comparison with the reference food.

duced a Code of Practice on nutrient claims in food labels and in advertisements. The preceding box provides a summary of the NFA's permitted claims and the criteria for these.

103. Use your local corner store rather than the shopping mall

Technology has brought marvellous changes to society—among them, the shopping mall. A mall in your neighbourhood means you can do all your business with one stop. And if you're lucky enough to win the fight for the closest car park to the exit, you may not have to move your legs much at all.

This is indeed what has been shown by Dr Billi Corti of the University of Western Australia in her doctoral thesis on the effects of the environment on physical activity levels in the community. Dr Corti has found that having a corner store rather than a supermarket or shopping mall in your neighbourhood, means that you have a six times greater chance of achieving the levels of physical activity recommended for health by the National Heart Foundation. It's unlikely to mean the dismantling of shopping malls, but if you've got the option, the corner store may mean you'll live longer, although perhaps poorer.

104. Recognise weight-loss gimmicks for what they are

The weight control field is rife with scams, fads and gimmicks, all designed to lighten the pocket rather than the waistline. If you can recognise the basic principles behind many of these products, you will be a lot closer to escaping the endless cycle of gain and loss.

Any or all of the following should be taken as an indication that a weight loss product or program is a rip-off.

- Use of the terms 'magic','wonder' or 'miracle' in promotions.
- Use of a 'new', 'secret' or 'unique' ingredient.
- Ingredients from inaccessible places, e.g. ocean floor, Tibetan mountains.
- Promise of dramatic weight loss in a short period of time.
- Promises of 'no effort', 'no exercise', 'no dieting'.
- Use of a white-coated person in promotions.
- Use of unconditional money-back guarantees if a certain weight loss is not achieved.
- Use of testimonials from 'cured' patients.
- Complicated (and usually unsupported) technical explanations of how the product works.

105. Watch out for the fattening effects of television

According to Dr Bill Dietz, a paediatric obesity specialist from the Boston Floating Hospital, television makes kids fat. Over 35% of American children now watch more than five hours of TV per day. Is it just coincidental that around 35% are now also overweight or obese?

Television has a number of effects on children that actually cause an increase in fatness.

Dietz suggests that it's not coincidence. Television, he says, has a number of effects on children that actually cause an increase in fatness. In the first place, it decreases the amount of physical activity they might otherwise carry out. There's also evidence that TV viewing may actually decrease the metabolic rate and lead to a greater than usual storage of body fat. Why this is so is not known. But the effect appears to be more than that created by the decrease in exercise.

Secondly, watching television can lead to an increase in food intake, due to the convenience of eating while viewing and an increase in the amount of snacking. It's also more likely that what's eaten will be high-fat snacks rather than healthy low-fat foods. Additionally, the influence of food advertising on TV is likely to further enhance the effect.

Dietz and others are now suggesting a decrease in TV time allowed for children to help prevent the early onset of obesity. 'A decrease in inactivity, by not sitting in front of a TV, may be one of the most effective ways of helping prevent childhood obesity,' says Dr Dietz.

106. Control your micro-environment

The environment in which we live can be broken into a number of different categories. In the first place, there's a division between the macro- and micro-environments. Secondly, there's a distinction between the physical and the socio-cultural environment. These classifications and some examples of each are shown in the figure opposite.

The macro-environment represents the global or national environment in which we live and the influences of such things as technology, advertising and social factors. It's generally difficult for any one individual to significantly influence the macro-environment.

The micro-environment includes your immediate physical environment, around the house, your local area, and your immediate social and workplace networks.

Changes in the micro-environment are vital to the maintenance of reduced body weight. Simple approaches are to keep fatty foods out of the house; not to keep or use effort-saving devices; and getting family and peer support for any weight control efforts. Control of the micro-environ-

ENVIRONMENTS INFLUENCING BODY WEIGHT MANAGEMENT

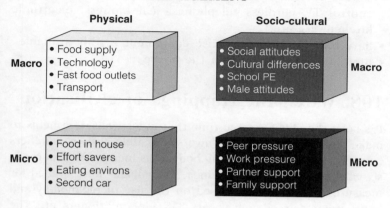

ment, particularly in our modern, energy reduced society, can be a vital part of any fat-loss program.

107. Try a 'home audit' to check your micro-environment

Changing the home environment can reduce the prospects for fat gain. The table below is a check list which can be used as an indicator for modifying this 'micro-environment'.

A 'home audit' for fat loss
Check the household for:
• high-fat foods (i.e. 10% fat) stored in the house
• accessibility of fatty snack foods and other 'treats'
• oversized meals presented at meal times
Try to ensure that you:
• buy low-fat alternative products, e.g. milk
• limit the fats or oils used in cooking
• use low-fat cooking methods and machines (i.e. microwaves, grillers)

- allow easy access to fresh fruit
- reduce excessive use of effort-saving devices (e.g. remote control TV, cordless telephones, leaf blowers, electronic kitchenware etc.)
- have bikes or other exercise equipment readily available
- limit eating places within the house

108. Watch the trappings of civilisation

It's been thought for some time that industrialisation helps to make populations fat. Now University of Melbourne researchers have proved this by measuring body mass index (BMI) scores in six villages in Papua New Guinea. The villages were graded for measures of 'modernity' based on the use of technology and effort-saving devices such as cars, TVs, air conditioners, etc. The villages were also graded on modernity of their housing, employment and education. As modernity indices increased, so did obesity, as measured by body mass index. Physical activity on the other hand decreased, as might be expected.

Having all the mod cons at your disposal may make life easier. But if they're all used all of the time, they can also make you much fatter.

109. Beware the fad diets that abound in the modern environment

The *Oxford Dictionary* defines a fad as a 'peculiar notion' or a 'craze'. This beautifully sums up fad diets. There are many which have come and gone over time. There are many others which are reincarnations of the old ones with a new gimmick or, in some cases, just a new cover on the book. Some fad diets incorporate a strategy that has some theoretical and potential merit, like chewing your food 100 times before swallowing. Of course this will slow down eating, which is a good idea, but maintaining such a practice in the long term is ridiculous.

Perhaps the most import evaluation of any diet is that it's possible to maintain it for life. Only an individual plan with some trial and error will accomplish this.

110. Have a plan to deal with social eating

Both rats and people eat more when they're in a group than when they're alone. There's much we don't know about what scientists call the 'cohabitation effect'. But recognising the social influences on individual food intake are the first step to drafting a plan to deal with them.

If you're aware that social eating—either with friends or at the in-laws—is likely to encourage either over-eating or eating the wrong types of foods, there are things you can do about it. Ask for smaller serves. Don't always feel you have to finish what is on the plate. Ask for more vegetables and less fat. Have an alternative to dessert, such as tea or coffee. Most of all, be prepared.

111. If you drink soft drink, go for the diet drinks

Each year the average Australian guzzles down about 80 litres of soft drink. Given that some people don't drink any, others must be making up the shortfall in copious quantities. If you have a soft spot for 'softies', consider the diet version of the real thing. There are considerable energy savings to be made with low-cal beverages.

One 375 mL can of regular soft drink contains about 10 teaspoons of sugar. Compare this with a drink which is artificially sweetened—the figure drops down to just a small pinch of sugar. While sugar itself is not the main problem, it's quite likely that it's taken in with a degree of fat, in which case the sugar will be used as energy and the fat will be stored in reserves, i.e. on the waist or the buttocks.

How do you get the sweetness without the sugar? Diet drinks have sugar substitutes which have no, or negligible, calories. If you don't like the taste of diet soft drinks, try a few different types. Some, like diet colas, can be made a bit more like the real thing just by adding a piece of lemon. Even better, just go for the old Adam's ale. Not only is water refreshing, it's also calorie free.

112. Don't sit while you can stand; don't ride when you can walk

The decline in incidental activity in modern Western life has significantly reduced daily energy expenditure. While a return to the pre-Industrial Revolution environment is unlikely, the addition of certain activities to daily living can compensate for part of the decline in overall energy expenditure.

- Don't sit when you can stand
- Don't drive or ride when you can walk
- Don't use remote controls for TVs, stereos, garage doors, etc.
- Do it yourself—don't ask someone else (i.e. the kids) to do it for you
- Mow the lawn and wash the dishes by hand
- Carry your bags—don't use a trolley
- Walk up stairs—don't use a lift or escalator
- Park away from your destination and walk
- Walk, don't drive, locally
- Hang out the clothes—don't use a clothes drier

113. Capitalise on modern food technology

The rise in the number and quality of lower fat foods on the market is testament to a fat-conscious society. But their effectiveness for fat loss is a hot topic for scientific debate. A 1994 study carried out in the United States caused some ripples when it showed that people eating low-fat foods over an extended time tend to compensate by just eating more.

However, a similar study carried out in the Netherlands recently showed no such effect. When given free access to full fat foods over a six month period, a group of over 100 people ate more fat (and more total energy) than a similar group given access to low-fat versions of the products. The decrease in fat in the diet of those on low-fat foods was around 7%, with no increase in fat taken in from other products that could be purchased from normal suppliers.

The adoption of reduced-fat foods as part of a low-fat diet therefore appears to have the desired effect in reducing total fat consumption, and at least in the short term will benefit fat loss. For long-term success, it may be wise to check for any extra compensation and even consider an increase in consumption of foods naturally low in fat, such as fruits and vegetables.

114. Substitute person-power for horsepower

Improvements in technology have been both a boon and a bane to modern societies. Using remote controls for televisions, garage doors and communications may make life more efficient, but they also make it less energetic. The decline in energy use is translated into a decrease in fat burned and hence an increase in body fat.

In 1995, Professor Phillip James of the Rowett Institute in Scotland calculated that although the average English person in the mid 1990s was eating approximately 750 kcals per day less than in 1970, they must also be burning around 800 kcals less in energy expenditure than in 1970 to have increased their body weight as much as they had over the period (i.e. about 1 g a day on average or 1 kg every three years). This can be translated to show that the average person in the 1990s is doing the equivalent of walking 10 km per day less than the average person in 1970—all through the grace of modern machinery!

The activities of the average person in the 1990s is equivalent to walking 10 km per day less than the average person in 1970.

   Professor James points out that because technology is not likely to disappear overnight, the only solution to this is a change in the physical environment which will encourage people to engage once more in the incidental activities that were once needed for day-to-day living: to use person-power instead of horsepower, to walk up stairs instead of catching an escalator, to park the car some distance from your destination and walk, and so on. Increases in incidental activity reduce the need for planned or otherwise institutionalised exercise.

115. Go for a treadmill: the best home exercise machine for losing fat

These days, partly in response to perceptions of decreased safety on the streets, the market for home exercise machines is booming. Home devices have always sold well, but in the past they've centred around weight-lifting machines or spurious 'flab fighting' devices.
   Now, with increased knowledge about the benefits of aerobic exercise, demand has changed to the more aerobic machines. These allow for continual use of the large muscle

groups over an extended period. New versions include tread-mills, stationary bicycles, stair climbers, rowing machines and simulated cross-country skiing machines.

All claim benefits over each other. But which has the evidence to prove it?

Researchers at the Medical College of Wisconsin have recently carried out the first unbiased scientific test, using six different machines with different experienced subjects at different time periods.

The machines analysed were an Airdyne bicycle machine with air-resistant wheel spokes, a standard cycle ergo-meter, a simulated cross-country skiing machine, a rowing ergometer, a stair climber and a treadmill for walking and running.

A treadmill results in up to 40% more energy being used at a set level of exertion than an exercise cycle.

All tests on the machines were standardised to a level of effort using a psychological measure known as the 'per-ceived rate of exertion' (PRE). This allows a subjective rating of effort on a scale of from 1 to 20. The rating used in these tests varied from 11 (fairly light) to 15 (hard). The actual energy use (per minute) was then estimated using standard physiological measures.

The researchers scored treadmills as the most energy effective machines. A treadmill results in up to 40% more energy being used at a set level of perceived exertion than an exercise cycle, which used the least energy. They did not, however, measure the effectiveness of the machines in achieving a heart rate range goal. For greatest economy of time and effort, the treadmill led the pack.

116. Exercise with a partner/friend

The biggest problem with any form of planned exercise in a weight management program is sticking with it. Psychologists have shown a number of factors increase your chances. Exercising with a friend or partner is one of them. Exercising with a partner can not only increase your adherence to a program, it can provide you with valuable feedback and support.

Having an arrangement to exercise with a partner makes it more difficult to renege when conditions are not ideal. A possible danger, however, is becoming so dependent on that partner that the program breaks down if the partner is not available. The 'buddy system' is therefore recommended to aid motivation, but you should also try to develop your own level of motivation.

5
BIOLOGICAL INFLUENCES

There are some things in life you can change, and some you can't. While biology falls into the latter category, a knowledge of some of the ways in which biological influences work on body weight may help you to understand why John and Joan find it easier than Mark and Mary to keep their weight under control.

In the first place there are genetic differences. While we have always known that we inherit characteristics from our parents, recent advances in molecular biology have actually found many of the genes which relate to body weight. By the mid 1990s, 23 genes had been specifically identified as associated with obesity. The scramble is now on to synthesise some of their products (proteins which usually have a 'signalling' role in the body) so a magic obesity-eliminating elixir can be produced in the form of a tablet. So far this has not happened, but science is full of surprises.

Gender is a second biological influence. Because of their important reproductive function, nature has granted females the privilege of storing and conserving energy-rich body fat more efficiently than males. Fat is also stored in different parts of the body in males and females and responds to attempts to reduce it in different ways. There are some tricks which may help to overcome women's propensity to store fat, but just the knowledge that this is caused by biology may be enough to allow women to feel more comfortable with their existing physical dimensions. Gender differences are also important for pregnancy and contraception.

A third biological factor considered here is ageing. Physiological changes associated with ageing make it easier to gain fat and more difficult to lose it as one gets older. Again, there are gender-based differences here, with older (post-menopausal) women shifting their pattern of body fatness from more on the lower body to more on the upper body. This, and other changes, make different techniques for body fat reduction and weight loss necessary at different stages in life. Some scientifically based approaches to this are considered below.

117. Accept (and understand) your physical limitations

A continued drive to achieve what may be physically impossible can lead to the kind of psychological problems associated with many weight control programs aimed at women. Everybody should be aware of their genetic limitations and be happy to work to these—including being comfortable at a higher than normal, but healthy, level of body fatness.

One way of accepting yourself is to understand just what overfatness is and how it can affect your health. The figure below shows one classification based on body mass index (BMI) measures, calculated by dividing weight by height squared (kg/m^2).

DEFINITIONS OF OVERFATNESS AND OBESITY

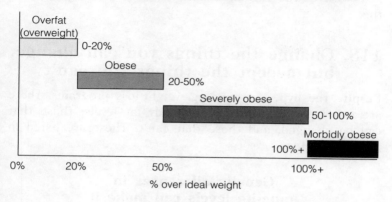

% over ideal weight

Recommendations for action for each of these categories is defined as follows:

Obesity category	General recommendations
Ideal (BMI 19–25)	Stay at the same weight
Overfat/overweight (BMI 25–30)	Eating counselling; behaviour therapy; movement management by trained fat-loss leader
Obese (BMI 30–40)	All of the above + medical supervision where appropriate
Severely obese (BMI 40–50)	Specialist medical referral; drug therapy; possible surgery + all the above
Morbidly obese (BMI 50+0)	Specialist medical referral; drug therapy; medically supervised very low calorie diet; surgery + all the above

As you can see, the severity of, and need for treatment within, each of these categories varies. Find your own level

and work to the recommendations to do something about
this.

118. Change the things you can change, but accept the things you can't

Despite the hype surrounding weight-loss programs, there
are two types of influences on body fat levels: those that
can be changed, and those that can't. These are listed in
the table below.

**Genetic diferences in
appetite levels can make it
much harder for one
person to resist food
than another.**

FACTORS INFLUENCING BODY FAT LEVELS

Things that can be changed		Things that can't be changed	
Food	Fat	Genetics	Fat/lean
	Sugar		Active/inactive
Drink	Alcohol	Level of obesity	Lean
	Soft drink		Overweight
	Fruit juice		Obese
Movement	Work	Age	Young
	Leisure		Middle aged
	Recreation		Old
Metabolism		Gender	Male
Habits			Female

Even within those things that can't be changed, there are
different levels of success for different individuals. Genetic
differences in appetite levels, for example, can make it much
harder for one person to resist food than another. Some of
the factors we've listed may be genetically determined (which

puts them among those things that can't be changed—at least as yet), while some may be behaviourally determined and so are able to be modified. The importance of individual differences is now much more readily recognised at the scientific level. People aren't always to blame for their excess fat.

119. Accept some increases in body fat with age

It's natural to add a little fat to the body with the increasing years—even as young as 40. The reasons for this, scientists think, are:

- Decreased sensitivity of fat cells to the hormones which stimulate fat breakdown (probably due to a decrease in the number of receptors on fat cells)
- Decreased overall metabolic rate
- Reduced muscle mass
- Decrease of a muscle protein that helps bind fat into muscle for use as energy
- Decreased spontaneous physical activity, or the activity normally carried out throughout the day
- Increased eating (although this is often under-reported)

The good news is that moderate fat gains with ageing don't appear to be as dangerous as those in the young. They can be worse, though, if the gains are too much (i.e. more than 8–9 kg over one's weight at age 20), so caution is still needed.

120. Understand the difference between biological and emotional hunger

There are two main types of hunger. The first is *biological*, or real, hunger. The second is *emotional*, or socially and psychologically influenced appetite. Recognition of the distinction is important because this can help you to stop over-eating.

Biological hunger is where:

- The hunger is genuinely physiological
- It doesn't go away if you wait (e.g. 15 minutes) before eating
- It increases over time
- Alternative distractions will not reduce the craving

In contrast, emotional hunger is where:

- The hunger is psychological rather than physiological
- It is likely to go away or decrease in intensity if you wait
- It doesn't increase over time
- Alternative distractions can reduce the craving

In modern societies, it's generally emotional hunger or *appetite*, rather than physiological hunger, that needs to be controlled. The implications of appetite for over-eating are most important. Fatty foods have a low level of satiation, but a high level of satiety. This means that more can be eaten at the time of eating without giving a feeling of fullness. High-carbohydrate and fibre-rich foods, on the other hand, have a high satiation, as well as a relatively high satiety, value. This means that you're likely to eat less at the time you're eating, because you feel full.

The implications are that a meal high in carbohydrate and fibre is likely to make you less hungry and less fat than a meal high in fat.

121. Be aware of racial differences in fat stores and fat loss

Among the factors known to influence weight loss, racial differences have probably been dealt with least. Yet simple observation reveals big differences in body shape between different racial groups.

Negroid women store fat more around the hips and buttocks; African Americans have been shown to lose fat less readily than white Americans. Asian women are known to have small hips, so a waist-to-hip ratio used as a measure of risk in Caucasians will not generally be relevant for them, because they will have scores more characteristic of men.

The pattern of deposition of fat can also differ among racial groups. It's thought that the Chinese, for example, first put fat on at the waist, before they fill out all over. Many Pacific island groups just seem to look at food and get fat—at least when that food is modern Western food. On their traditional diets they're still big people, but their fat is stored more evenly over the body, meaning a lower health risk.

With the intermixing of the world's peoples, different rates and locations of fat gain and loss are likely to become less predictable in the long term. In the meantime science is making us more aware of the reality of racial distinctions. It may require a quick trip to the family tree in the future to see just how and if fat loss can occur and how easy it will be.

122. Ignore the suggestion that a gut is a sign of manliness

For some men, manhood is reflected in a pot belly: a beer gut, as it's often known, says 'you're one of the boys'.

So here's some startling news. Extra fat around the stomach, and particularly around the organs of the trunk, could be associated with a *decrease* in testosterone—that well known male hormone often touted as the indicator of manhood.

Research indicates that levels of the male hormone testosterone are inversely related to gut size.

Testosterone is real male. It's secreted by the gonads (testes) and is clearly associated with the typical symbols of masculinity—deep voice, hair on the face, more muscle, more aggression. It also appears to tell the body how to use up fat in the fat stores of the body.

Professor Per Bjorntorp, a leading Swedish physiologist, has followed radioactive fat in food in the bodies of castrated rats, some of which were supplemented with testosterone and some not, and compared this to normal male rats. Those with active testosterone tended to 'use up' the fat much more readily than those with low testosterone, who tended to store it more in fat cells.

It's known that fat men also have reduced testosterone levels. What is cause and what is effect is not clear. What is clear is that a pot belly is, in hormonal terms, just the opposite of what's thought of as a 'real man'.

123. Understand the limitations of exercise for weight loss in women

In the shadows of the 1980s fitness boom, it's almost heresy to suggest that exercise won't lead to fat loss. But this is now the opinion of several scientists, at least in relation to exercise in women. It could help explain the extreme difficulties some women have in trimming down—even with regular pounding of the pavement.

The exercise debate was stirred by a review in the *Journal of the American College of Nutrition*, in which exercise scientist Dr Gilbert Gleim showed that in a range of research studies with women, most show only limited effects of exercise on weight loss, particularly when compared with men. Gleim's conclusion: 'As an isolated weight loss modality . . . exercise should not be counted on to produce desired weight reductions [in women] unless the woman is committed to many hours of exercise a day'.

We don't know exactly why this is so. But some suggestions are:

- *Errors in dietary reporting*: Women tend to under-estimate the increase in food intake which seems to occur as a result of an increase in exercise. Men have been regularly shown to lose weight while training, even with an increase in food intake.

- *Body size and fitness*: Men's greater size and greater muscle mass mean that a man will use more energy to walk or run the same distance as a woman, even if they do it at the same relative intensity. For example, an average sized man will use about 40% more energy walking a kilometre than an average sized woman.

- *Fat cell differences*: Male and female fat cells have different densities of the receptors (male cells have more) which respond to hormones influencing fat burning (lypolysis) and storage (lipogenesis). These hormones, particularly those from the adrenal glands, are largely responsible for the fat-burning effects of exercise.

- *Body fat distribution*: Women tend to store fat around the hips and buttocks, whereas men store it more on the stomach. Lower body fat is known to be much more resistant to fat loss in general, and even more so in response to energy losses (e.g. exercise, diet), than upper body fat cells.

- *Sex steroid differences*: Female hormones may specifically prevent loss of body fat in the hip and buttock regions when the going gets tough in order to preserve energy for the biologically important function of childbirth.

**Recent research shows that
if food intake is restricted
too much in women,
resistance to fat loss can
increase even further.**

This is not to suggest that exercise is useless for weight control (or for good health in general) in women. If combined with reduced food intake it can be effective. However, other recent research shows that if food intake is restricted too much in women (e.g. to around 50% of the daily requirements), resistance to fat loss can increase even further. Very long duration, slower activities (e.g. walking for up to one hour a day) are likely to be best for women serious about fat loss.

124. Put on *an appropriate amount* of weight during pregnancy

The old saying of 'eating for two' may pose problems in pregnancy for women who are prone to gaining weight. Researchers from the Obesity Unit at the Karolinska Institute in Sweden examined this by studying obese women to see if their weight gain was connected with pregnancy. In 128 obese women studied, 73% had retained 10 kg or more in connection with a pregnancy. In another study of 1428 normal weight women, only 14% gained more than 5 kg after a pregnancy.

Normal weight gain during pregnancy, according to the Swedish researchers, is around 12.5 kg. From 3–6 kg of this is maternal adipose tissue designed to provide energy for the child during lactation. But this may only be needed if food is not readily available during lactation—a rare occurrence in affluent societies.

Women who gained more than 5 kg after delivery in the Swedish study were more likely to:

- Have had larger initial weight
- Have larger weight gain during pregnancy
- Have given up smoking
- Have less structured eating habits
- Be less likely to eat breakfast and lunch

- Eat larger meals and snack more, and
- Have less leisure time/physical activity after pregnancy

Contrary to other studies, the women's age and the number of pregnancies had little or no effect on weight gain. The researchers claim that although a low birth weight is a risk associated with gaining too little weight, this should be balanced against the adverse effects of overweight and obesity. The baby's birth weight doesn't seem to increase after a maternal weight gain of more than 10 kg. Thus, as birth weight increases up to a certain level and then plateaus, it may not be necessary to 'over eat for two'.

125. Take special care after two or more pregnancies

For many women each successsive pregnancy means another increase in weight, although this is by no means universal. Women in low socio-economic areas of Mexico City, for example, were recently found to increase their body weight significantly after giving birth to two or more children. The age of the mother was also important, with older mothers likely to gain more weight.

Whether this is caused by a natural phenomenon or changes in lifestyle patterns is difficult to assess. However, it's generally conceded that the women who record the biggest gains during pregnancy are likely to maintain a greater body weight afterward.

Thus, women should try not to gain too much weight after giving birth, and be wary of the effects of changes in activity levels and increased food intake associated with the stresses inherent in early childhood rearing.

126. Breastfeed (if you're a mother)

Female body fat stores are specifically designed to provide energy for childbirth and rearing. Estimates of the energy cost of breastfeeding show that the daily energy required is 300–400 kcals. Any deficit which can't be made up from excess food intake is supplied from the body's fat stores which, under non-lactating circumstances, are difficult to mobilise.

Research carried out in New York has shown that mothers who breastfeed for six months or longer stay leaner for up to two years than mothers who don't breastfeed. Mothers who breastfeed, and who eat up to 300 kcals a day more than non-breastfeeding mothers, tend to lose more weight in the six months after giving birth than non-breastfeeding mothers on a special diet and exercise program.

127. Choose a low dose contraceptive pill

Acceptance of the contraceptive pill in its early days was hampered by reports that it caused weight gain in young women. Scientific advances since have meant that lower doses of hormones are used in the pill, which presumably reduced the risk of weight gain.

This perception was recently put to the test in Israel with low dose oestrogen contraceptives. Body measures indicating fat distribution, as well as weight changes, were monitored in a number of women using the medication over three and six treatment cycles. No impact on weight, body composition or fat distribution was found in those using the pill compared to those not, suggesting that women on low oestrogen contraceptives need not worry about weight gain.

128. Be mindful of the menopause

The body fat and fat distribution of pre-menopausal women is known to be influenced largely by the female hormones, particularly oestrogen. After menopause, women lose the benefit of these hormones and fat stores begin to equate more with those of males. There is an increase in upper body fat, unfortunately not matched by a decrease in fat in those cells already established in the lower body.

Fat from the upper body, as with men, is more mobile than fat from the lower body, and hence older women are able to manage their extra fat stores with extra energy output and control over food, particularly fat intake. It's important for older women to be aware of the changes which occur naturally with the menopause so they can take action against them.

129. Don't be scared of HRT and weight gains in menopause

Hormone replacement therapy (HRT) is an attempt to re-store female hormone levels during menopause. This has been shown to reduce the incidence of heart disease in post-menopausal women, particularly in those with a family history of the problem. The association of heart disease with abdominal fat stores means that HRT, in helping older women to reduce upper body fat levels, may also be protect-ing them from heart disease.

These suggestions have not been convincingly proven in research carried out to date, possibly because of the varying mix of hormones in different HRT medications and women's idiosyncratic responses. Some research has shown a positive effect of HRT on body weight levels, but more needs to be done. At present it seems HRT may make it easier for older women to keep their body fat levels down.

130. Don't be afraid to pump a bit of iron as you get older

There's controversy about the benefits of weight training in body fat loss. Some exercise scientists suggest it may be better than other forms of exercise, such as walking, because it helps maintain, or even increase, muscle mass.

This in turn can add to the metabolic rate (because muscle is 'active'), and thus, theoretically at least, burn more energy.

In practice, the answer is less clear. Several studies using weight training have found no effect on body fat loss. Others find an effect, but only in certain people such as younger men. It's also questionable whether the time spent in weight training may be better spent carrying out more fat burning aerobic activity.

Several groups of researchers have tested the effects of weight training on older men and women, all groups showing improvements in strength and fitness. Weight loss effects have been less obvious, but this may be because of the increases in appetite that have gone with the programs. In any case, there is some support for the use of weight training with ageing for maintenance of body composition.

131. Beware of compensatory over-eating

The human body is exceedingly cunning about retaining body fat, even in the presence of increased energy expenditure. Because fat is a valuable energy source which can help you survive in times of low food availability, the body tries hard to preserve the fat it has. In essence, it's saying to you, 'I'm all right at this weight, thank you. At least I'm alive, and I've got some spare energy just in case I need it. For that reason I'm going to fight hard to keep it.'

Female humans, like female rats, tend to over-eat after exercise to compensate for the energy burned up, whereas male humans, more like male rats, tend to simply decrease their body weight.

One of the mechanisms by which this occurs is in energy compensation. In active people, food intake tends to increase to compensate for the energy used up during exercise. Athletes, for example, eat up to four times as much as non-active people, extra food which they burn off during exercise. Non-athletes may be a little less well regulated and may even balance their energy output by extra food input, thus maintaining a higher than wanted level of body fat.

The problem is worse in females. Swedish researchers in the 1980s found that female humans, like female rats, tend to over-eat after exercise to compensate for the energy burned up, whereas male humans, more like male rats, tend to simply decrease their body weight. More recently the same result has been found in human subjects in research carried out at Leeds University in the United Kingdom.

Particular attention may need to be paid to over-eating when an exercise regime is introduced into any weight management program, but whether such attention can overcome the biological drive to eat to maintain body fat, particularly in the case of women whose body fat reserves are required for the needs of reproduction, is not clear.

132. Beware of the 'bounce back' effect

Traditionally, fat cells have been thought to be relatively inert with little communication with other cells of the body. However, recent research has established that fat cells could have a hormonal function, with interactive communication with the eating centres in the brain.

It's been known for some time that the ex-obese tend to have a higher level of hunger than those who have never been obese, and it's now thought that this may be because fat cells that have been reduced in size send a message to the brain increasing hunger so they can return to their original size. For this reason, losing weight—particularly for the obese—is no guarantee of a lifetime of slenderness. A proper maintenance program incorporating all aspects of care needs to be taken to prevent the bounce back effect.

133. Don't wait up for the magic pill

The discovery of the *ob* gene and its product leptin, in 1994, gave obesity researchers hope of a quick solution in the form of a leptin-type drug to overcome hunger in those prone to obesity. But the actual situation appears to be becoming more complex the more research unravels it.

Although administration of leptin to obese strains of mice does appear to reduce their body weight drastically, measurement of leptin levels in humans shows that obese people already have *more* rather than *less* of this hormone (as was expected from a mutation of the gene which codes for the substance). This implies that the problem may not lie with the making of the hormone (i.e. the 'key'), but with a lack of the receptors (i.e. the 'locks') on which it acts.

Initially it was thought there would only be one type of receptor, which would be found in the appetite centre of the brain (hypothalamus). New studies, however, have found receptors in several other organs of the body. If these are deficient in the obese, one way of making them respond to leptin may be to develop an agonist drug (one which helps the 'key' fit in the 'lock').

Currently there's a flurry of research activity in this area. But knowing the complexity unravelled so far, it may not be wise to wait up for the results. We'll tell you in the morning!

134. Check your genetic limitations

Although not a guaranteed measure of heritability, your score on the following test can give you an indication of whether genes influence your weight level and why weight loss may be so difficult for you.

1. As far as you know, were either or both of your parents significantly overweight for most of their lives?

	Score
Neither/don't know	0
Yes, one parent	1
Yes, both parents	2

2. Do you have any brothers or sisters who have been significantly overweight for most of their lives?

No	0
Yes, one	1
Yes, more than one	2

3. When did you first become overweight?

After 20	0
During my teens	1
Before my teens	2

4. How difficult do you find it to take off weight?

Not difficult at all	0
Reasonably difficult	1
Very difficult	2

5. Where do you mainly get fat when you put on weight?

On the stomach	0
On the hips and buttocks	1
All over	2

Scores:

0–4: No apparent genetic involvement.

5–7: Moderate hereditary component.

8–10: There appears to be a significant hereditary component to your weight problem. This means you may need special help for effective weight loss.

135. Make sure your medications are not working against you

Some medicines have weight gain as a side effect. If this is the case, your doctor may be able to prescribe alternatives. Check the table below for any medications you may be using.

PRESCRIBED MEDICATIONS WHICH MAY AFFECT FAT OR WEIGHT LOSS

Androgens (male hormones)

Generic name:	Brand name:
ethyloestrenol	Orabolin
fluroxymesterone	Halotestin
nandrolone	Durabolin
oxymetholone	Adroyd
	Anapolon
stanozolol	Winstrol
testosterone	Andriol
	Primoteston
	Sustanon

Benzodiazepines (anti-anxiety)

Generic name:	Brand name:
alprozolam	Xanax
chlordiazepoxide	Librium
clorozepate	Tranxene
diazepam	Valium
lorazepam	Ativan
oxazepam	Serapax
flurazepam	Dalmane
temazepam	Normison
triazolam	Halcion
nitrazepam	Mogadon

Corticosteroids (anti-allergy; anti-inflammatory)

Generic name:	Brand name:
betamethasone	Celestone
dexamethasone	Decadron
cortisone (naturally occurring)	Cortate
hydrocortisone	Cortef
methylprednisolone	Medrol

prednisolone	Delta-Cortef
prednisone	Deltasone
triamcinolone	Aristocort

Cyproheptadines (allergy relief)
Generic name: *Brand name:*
cyproheptadine HCl   Periactin

Anti-diabetic agents
Generic name: *Brand name:*
(a) Insulin   Actrapid
      Humulin
      Velosulin
      Promatime
      Ultralente

(b) Sulfonylureas
   chlorpropamide   Diabinese
   glipizide   Minidiab
   tolbutamide   Rastinon

Phenothiazines (anti-psychotics)
Generic name: *Brand name:*
chlorpromazine   Largactil
prochlorperazine   Stemetil

Tricyclic anti-depressants
Generic name: *Brand name:*
amitriptyline   Endep
      Tryptanol
clomipramine   Anafranil
dothiepin   Prothiaden
imipramine   Tofranil

Oral contraceptives*
Type of pill (oestrogen content):   *Brand name (examples):*
Combined (30 µg and under)   Microgynon 30
      (35 µg)   Brevnor
      Modicon

	Nordette
(50 μg)	Microgynon 50
	Neogynon
	Orthornovum
	Ovulen
Phased (30–50 μg)	Biphasil
	Synphasic
	Triquilar

Hormone replacement therapy (HRT) medications*

Generic name: *Brand name:*

(a) Oestrogen
     conjugated oestrogens   Premarin
     ethinyloestradiol   Estigyn
                          Primogyn C
     oestradiol   Oestradiol implants

(b) Progesterone
     levonorgestrel   Microlut
                          Microval
     medroxyprogesterone   Depo-Provera
     norethisterone   Micronor
                          Primalut

* Some of these medications may cause fat gain in some women only.

6

BEHAVIOURAL INFLUENCES

Much excess fatness results from psychological causes, ranging from lack of self-esteem or self-confidence to reactions to early sexual and physical abuse. These can't be dealt with through simple admonitions to do more of, or less of, something, as we've listed here. They require detailed and usually prolonged counselling. However, some issues uncovered in recent research may help anyone overcome some of the behavioural negatives that act against weight loss. Some of these are based on sound laboratory research, but behaviour, by its nature, is often difficult to quantitatively assess. Some of the proposals in this section therefore come from psychological theories, albeit well accepted ones. Further references are included where possible to enable you to follow up points of particular interest.

136. Recognise that there are no quick easy fixes

Putting on and taking off weight is a gradual thing. Even under the most extreme conditions there's only so much

" I DIDN'T KNOW WHICH DIET TO CHOOSE SO I TOOK THE LOT."

that can be gained or lost in a set time period. Changes in the body's metabolism and other adaptive factors help to guarantee that this is the case, otherwise human beings wouldn't have survived the feasts and famines of the past.

Among commercial weight control programs there's almost a competition to see which can advertise the greatest weight loss in the shortest period of time. This approach is highly unethical and can ultimately lead to greater weight gains than losses—which, of course, would satisfy many commercial organisations because it would guarantee a continuous clientele.

Weight losses of more than 0.5–1 kg per week are now regarded as potentially counter-productive. Any suggestion of quick, easy fixes that can ensure this type of loss over the long term should be dismissed for their potential ill effects.

137. Don't expect big changes overnight

The average human body contains between 30–50 billion fat cells. Each of these contains around 0.5 micrograms of fat, making a total of around 15 kg of fat in the average person.

Even with maximal effort (i.e. eating yourself stupid and lying motionless), a weight gain of more than about 1 kg per week is difficult—after all, this represents nearly 10% of a body fat level which the body has often taken a lifetime to achieve. It stands to reason that body fat is unlikely to increase at a much greater rate.

Of course weight losses greater than this are possible. But most of the weight lost will be water, which is quickly regained. Significant decreases in weight will also lead to adaptive changes in metabolism which serve to slow the weight loss down and ultimately restore the body to its previous level.

Research has shown that ideal body weight losses for long-term maintenance are around 0.5–1.0 kg per week. Losses of 1.5 kg per week or more have been shown to increase the risk of health problems such as gallstones. They can also increase the risk of extra fatness—at a later time.

138. Make sure you're genuinely motivated

Motivation is the key to success in any weight management program. Rate yourself on the little test below to see if you're really ready to try to lose fat. Compare your score with those at the end.

Measuring motivation

1. Compared to previous attempts, how motivated are you this time to lose fat?

1	2	3	4	5
Not at all motivated				Extremely motivated

2. How certain are you that you'll stay committed to a fat-loss program for the time it will take to reach your goal?

1	2	3	4	5
Not at all certain				Extremely certain

3. Considering all outside factors at this time in your life—the stress you may be feeling, your family obligations etc.—to what extent can you tolerate the effort required to stick to a fat reduction plan?

1	2	3	4	5
Cannot tolerate				Can tolerate easily

4. Think honestly about how much fat you hope to lose and how quickly you hope to lose it. Figuring a weight loss of around 0.5–1.0 kg per week, how realistic is your expectation?

1	2	3	4	5
Not at all realistic				Extremely realistic

5. While dieting, do you fantasise about eating a lot of your favourite foods?

1	2	3	4	5
Always	Frequently	Occasionally	Rarely	Never

6. How confident are you that you can work regular exercise into your daily schedule, starting tomorrow?

1	2	3	4	5
Not at all confident				Extremely confident

Scores:

6–12: You're not very serious about losing fat. You should leave it until you are.

13–24: You're reasonably motivated. But you may need some help.

25+: Your motivation is high. You should have little trouble getting started.

139. Become aware of your eating 'habits'

Much eating occurs from the association of a cue (e.g. ads on TV) with a reward (e.g. getting up to get something to eat or drink). After the association between the stimulus and the response becomes automatic, the habit is carried out, often without conscious awareness.

The first stage of reducing this, says psychologist and author Hilary Tupling, is to 'stalk' the habit, 'like a hunter stalks his prey', to understand it, then break the link between the cue and the reward. This can be done by replacing the reward with another, more helpful reward (e.g. doing some exercises during ad breaks), or removing the cue (e.g. turning the TV off).

To apply this to your eating behaviour: first, stalk your habit, identify and write down what it is that makes you eat more, or more often, when you eat and how you feel when you eat at those times. Second, once identified, try to break the stimulus–response connection by associating another response with the stimulus (e.g. feeling depressed, feeling angry, an ad on TV, etc.) that has automatically led to the eating response.

Becoming aware of habits is often enough to help you break those habits.

140. Don't believe yourself—particularly if you're the diet-resistant type

'Diet resistant' is a term given to people who seem to never lose weight, even as a response to reduced food intake. It's a common phenomenon often put down to 'gland problems' or 'genetics'.

Diet resisters have usually been taken at their word. They *say* they don't eat much, and they *do* exercise. But now evidence indicates that not only the over-weight, but also normal weight, people tend to under-estimate the amount of food they eat and over-estimate the amount of exercise they do. This could help explain why those who don't think they can lose weight, really don't seem able to.

Working with a group of obese individuals in New York, scientists used a radio-active monitoring technique to accurately estimate the amount of energy taken in (food) and burned up (exercise), over a two week period. All of those measured had been on a self-reported food intake of less than 1200 kcals per day over the previous six months but had failed to lose any weight.

Compared with their actual energy use, as measured radioactively, the 'diet-resistant' overweight under-estimated their daily food intake by around 30% and over-estimated the amount of energy they burned up each day by almost 40%.

The implications of this are that the apparently 'diet-resistant' need to pay particular care to estimating their food and exercise levels. If possible, more accurate techniques of estimation, such as a daily diet diary and exercise log or pedometer for measuring exercise output, should be used.

141. Beware of the 'three Ds'

In his book *Act Thin, Stay Thin*, Dr Richard Stuart explains that we often confuse what we would like to do with what we actually do. Stuart lists three sources of delusion which can explain why some people sometimes over-eat and under-exercise without necessarily realising it:

1. *Denial:* Helps us maintain a positive image of ourselves. With eating, the main form of denial is denying you ate

too much. With exercise, it's denying that you *don't* do enough regular activity. The usual response is, 'I'm on my feet all day'. Dealing with denial requires honest understanding as well as some objective measurements (pedometer scores, food diaries, etc.) that can't be denied.

2. *Distraction:* Occurs when other things are happening. It's easier to eat too much, for example, while having a drink or talking with friends. Research has shown that overweight people are more vulnerable to distractions than normal weight people. When obese and non-obese people are left in a room with open access to food, and with a clock in view which is sped up so that 50 minutes represents an hour, fat people eat when they think it's *time* to eat (e.g. at 1 pm, although it may really only be 12 pm). Non-fat people eat *when they feel hungry*. They're not distracted by the time.

3. *Distortion:* Refers to the way big people judge their behaviour. Studies measuring *actual* food intake and exercise output against *reported* food intake and exercise output have shown that overweight people under-estimate food intake and over-estimate exercise. This is not thought to be deliberate (because even normal weight people do it). It's an unrecognised *distortion* of the facts. They're just unaware of the amount they actually eat.

Self-monitoring can help reduce the triple threats of denial, distraction and distortion because, according to Dr Stuart, '. . . you cannot make sound plans for effective behaviour change when you start from where you think you'd like to be instead of where you really are'.

142. Learn optimism

In the late 1960s, Dr Martin Seligman and his colleagues at the University of Pennsylvania found that rats that were given electric shocks over which they had no control actually learned to be helpless—they became timid, weak and diseased and some even died. Rats that were shocked, but had a chance to learn how to control the shock, on the other hand, actually flourished.

Since the 1970s, Seligman and his students have turned to clinical psychology to try to work out how learned helplessness could be converted to learned optimism. Seligman's theory is based on a branch of psychology called cognitive therapy. His findings help to explain a well known phenomenon in weight control—why people who fail continue to fail—and what might be done about it.

In humans learned helplessness develops, according to Seligman, not because things go wrong, but because of what we *think about* things going wrong. Everyone suffers setbacks in life, but different people—pessimists and optimists—have different ways of looking at them.

The common characteristics that lead pessimists to helplessness and depression are the three Ps—personalisation, permanence and pervasiveness:

1. *Personalisation:* For the pessimist, everything that happens is '*my fault—I broke the diet because I'm weak*', rather than '*it's a totally unrealistic diet and I was seduced by advertising*'. This can only be overcome by externalising i.e. not blaming oneself.
2. *Permanence:* When something goes wrong for an optimist it's unfortunate, but a temporary setback. A pessimist, on the other hand, is convinced that this is something that always happens; it's a lifetime disaster—'*I always fail because I've got no self control*'. By re-thinking problems from the permanent to the temporary ('*I had no self control today*'), pessimism can be overcome, according to Seligman.
3. *Pervasiveness:* This implies that even small things that go wrong pervade the pessimist's life ('*I spilt the tea, therefore I'm a failure, therefore there's no point in try-*

ing'). Everyone suffers small setbacks, but the optimist sees these for what they are: small, isolated problems.

The thought patterns of personalisation, permanence and pervasiveness in pessimists are maintained, according to Seligman, by 'rumination', or mulling over the bad things continually, but not necessarily doing the same for the good things. The pessimist who has learned helplessness is therefore set up for failure in weight control. It's little wonder these people bounce from diet to diet with little chance of success.

Seligman's process of cognitive therapy for reversing the cycle of learned helplessness involves four stages:

1. Recognising your thoughts at the times you feel worst: These can be in the form of quick phrases or sentences (e.g. *'I can never lose weight. I've got no self control'*).
2. Learning to dispute these automatic thoughts by marshalling contrary evidence: Based on reversing the three Ps of pessimism, this involves making bad thoughts temporary, external and non pervasive.
3. Learning to make different explanations, called re-attributions, to dispute automatic thoughts: *'I ate that cake today, but I felt obliged to, and I can walk it off later'*.
4. Learning how to displace depressing thoughts: This can be done by using processes such as thought stopping (see Tip 143).

143. Use thought-stopping techniques to distract yourself from disruptive thinking

The art of thought stopping is now used widely by psychologists to help people relearn negative thinking patterns. Some thought-stopping techniques to help weight watchers include:

1. Slamming the palm of your hand against a fixed object such as a wall, and saying to yourself, 'Stop', before thinking about something else.
2. Imagining a large roadside Stop sign in your mind. Concentrate on the details of this every time a negative thought enters your head (such as in the middle of the night).
3. Examining very closely a small object you might pick up in your hand. Note the curves, material, irregularities and otherwise unobvious aspects of the object.
4. Wearing a rubber band around your wrist which you snap every time a negative thought occurs, then changing the thought to be less permanent, pervasive or personal.
5. Using worry beads or something similar that you can carry in your hand or pocket. Concentrate on the feel of each individual object instead of thinking negative thoughts.

144. Think rationally

Habits can be behavioural or cognitive. Bad behavioural habits are incorrect ways of acting. Bad cognitive habits are incorrect ways of thinking. Both can lead to negative outcomes in relation to weight control; behavioural habits through actions that lead directly to incorrect eating or ways of moving, thought habits through thought patterns that lead indirectly to eating for comfort, stress reduction or as reward.

Cognitive habits can lead to cyclical processes of thinking. An example might be the way one thinks about bingeing to excess on a particular occasion. A rational way of thinking about this would be to realise that it was just one occasion and not likely to have any lasting effect. Irrational thought processes might lead people to think they are failures, that they must never binge and that, as a result, they are depressed. An obvious consequence of depression is to seek comfort through tasty, sweet and/or fatty foods. Hence the cycle is perpetuated.

American psychologist Albert Ellis pioneered a process called rational emotive therapy, or RET, to deal with irrational thinking. Basically, RET involves disputing irrational beliefs to come up with alternative consequences. According to Ellis, the most damaging consequences result from the irrational beliefs that one 'must', 'should' or 'have to' think in some way. RET is a technique designed to help combat this process.

The ABCD of RET

According to Albert Ellis, everyone is faced with Adversity at some stage during their lives. This may be large or trivial. Over the years we develop Beliefs to cope with adversity; these may be real or imaginary. The type of belief we have leads to Consequences, which can be negative (*I'm not good at sport therefore I'm not good at anything*). Over time, these can build up a feeling of learned helplessness. The sequence needs to be Disputed at the belief stage and beliefs turned to learned optimism if successes like a reduction in body fat are to occur over the long term.

This is the ABCD of learned optimism: Adversity leads to a Belief which has Consequences. Negative Beliefs need to be Disputed or Disrupted to break the chain of 'learned helplessness'. This occurs by changing thought patterns (and thereby beliefs) by Disputation, or arguing the point with yourself based on reversing the three Ps of pessimism, or Distraction of negative thoughts through thought-stopping techniques (see Tip 143).

145. Give yourself permission to eat

Social pressures to attain an unrealistic body image are strong. Many people, women in particular, have suffered from years of social pressure to attain an unrealistic body, exemplified, in many cases, by almost anorexic fashion models. As a result, they often feel guilty and depressed when they succumb to pressures to over-eat, or indeed to eat anything they think may be in the least bit fattening.

As shown in the diagram below, guilt is a counter-productive emotion in regard to weight control. Guilt often leads to over-eating because eating was established early in life as a comfort for depression and anxiety—how many times were you given sweets to comfort you when you were upset about something?

THE VICIOUS CYCLE OF OBESITY
(after Wysoker, 1994)

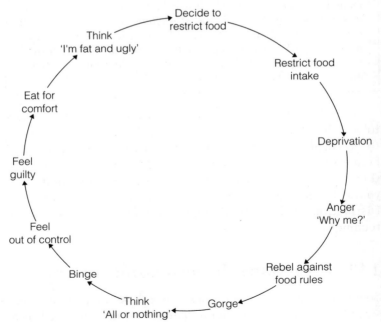

Guilt is a
counter-productive emotion
in regard to weight control.

With many people for whom guilt is a problem, the first
stage in a proper weight management program is to develop
a sensible attitude to food by giving yourself permission to
eat, to *occasionally* over-eat, to eat tempting sweet and fatty
foods sometimes, and to *enjoy* the process of eating. This
can help break the guilt cycle which is often the cause of
the obesity problem.

146. Sort out your emotional problems
before you try to sort out your
weight

Obesity and overweight can result from emotional disturbances such as stress, grief or bereavement. These situations
can often lead to comfort eating and inactivity. But taking
these crutches away is likely only to make the situation
worse: the chances of failure are increased and the prospects
for future weight loss diminished.

Instead of trying to 'hold onto your hat in a cyclone',
it may be better to deal with the issues causing the cyclone.
The primary cause of the problem is likely to be the emotional disturbance. This should be dealt with through
counselling, help from your social networks or psychological
assistance before any concerted attempt is made to do
anything about body weight. Become relaxed in your life and
you'll become relaxed about your weight.

147. Avoid saunas and other heat
treatments for weight loss

Heat treatments such as saunas and steam baths have often
been used as weight-loss techniques. The problem is, the

loss is purely in the form of water lost through sweat, which is quickly replaced on rehydration.

A principal aim of the body is homeostasis, or the maintenance of a median physiological position. Core body temperature is maintained at around 37.5°C and the body will work hard to maintain this temperature in the presence of external cooling or heating.

Much less effort is required to cool the body down than to heat it. In fact, in the presence of excess heat there is a tendency to slow down to conserve energy and maintain body temperature. In the presence of cold, on the other hand, the body is stimulated to use up a good deal of energy to raise body temperature.

Heat treatments like sauna baths may be relaxing, but they have no long-term effect on body weight.

For this reason the ideal treatment for fat loss would not be heat treatments like saunas and steam baths, but cold treatments like an ice-box or refrigerated room. Unfortunately (or fortunately), there's little chance of these selling in the average fitness centre. Heat treatments are pleasant, and can have relaxation and other psychological benefits, but they have no long-term effect on weight loss.

148. Go mild with your energy restriction

There's been a lot of research carried out in recent years on the weight-loss effects of very low-calorie diets (less than 1000 kcal) with very big people. In general, the results have been disappointing, with later weight gain often making up for the small losses that are made. Ironically, there's been little research using mild energy restriction in individuals who are not drastically overweight.

This was the basis of some recent research carried out in the Netherlands. Nutrition scientists reduced the total energy input in a small group of men by 20% after determining how much food was needed daily to keep them at a stable weight. They compared their weight loss over a ten week period with a control group of men who kept eating the amount of food required to keep them stable.

> **Small changes in food intake are likely to be much better for fat loss than drastic changes over the long term.**

The reduction in food in the test group resulted in an average food intake of around 2200 kcals/day—a not insubstantial amount to keep going on. Still, the men lost an average of 7.4 kg, over 83% of which was body fat. Perhaps more importantly, there was no plateauing out of weight loss over the ten weeks of study. The implications are that small changes in food intake are likely to be much better for fat loss than drastic changes over the long term, even though your head may tell you otherwise.

149. Watch what you over-eat when you think you're under-eating

Low-fat and low-calorie foods are now relatively easy to come by. But some American research has shown that these foods might have an unexpected effect on total food intake.

Studying women who were given a pre-load of food (i.e. the equivalent of a first course), scientists found that the amount of food eaten later in the meal depended on whether the pre-load was labelled high fat or low fat—irrespective of whether the label was accurate. Those eating what they thought was a low-fat pre-load tended to eat more at the main meal than those who thought they were eating a high-fat pre-load, or had no information about the fat content.

Unexpectedly, there was no difference in the amount of food eaten after the pre-load between women labelled restrained, or non-restrained eaters. The indications are that messages about the content of a food can influence the actual energy intake of that food—at least in some women.

150. Make sure that what you think about food is actually true

The taste, or even the *predicted* taste, of a food can encourage greater over-eating. Hence, whether a person *thinks* a food is likely to be filling or not may be important in determining just how much he or she eats.

This notion was recently put to the test by psychologists at Leeds University in England. A number of people were asked to rate how tasty and filling they thought were a number of different types of foods, particularly snack foods. They were then given these to eat, and their food intake for the rest of the day monitored to see if their ratings of 'fillingness' conformed to the ability of the food to satisfy hunger.

> **Whether a person thinks a food is likely to be filling or not, may be important in determining just how much he or she eats.**

High-sweet and high-fat snack foods (e.g. chocolate, pastries) were generally thought to be highly filling, but they led to almost double the total daily energy consumption of other lower-sweet or lower-fat foods. In other words, they were less 'filling' than they appeared, leading to greater food intake. This suggests that some over-eating might occur because the eye deceives the stomach. With fattening food, not all is as it may look.

151. Don't assume you'll automatically put on weight if you quit smoking

Researchers in California have studied weight gain by ex-smokers in a large sample of identical and non-identical twins from the biggest twin register of births in the world, those born between 1917 and 1927. They followed over 2000 who had quit smoking and compared the weight gains in this group with a matched number of ex-smokers and non-smokers.

Contrary to popular belief, almost as many smokers either lose weight or remain stable, as those who gain weight after quitting smoking.

The quitters were then divided into four categories: those who gained over 11.3 kg or more over 16 years since quitting (super-gainers); those who gained more than 2.3 kg but less than 11.3 kg (gainers), those with no weight change (weight stable), and those who actually lost weight (weight losers). The percentages in each group compared to continuing smokers and non-smokers were:

	Quitters	Non-smokers	Continuing smokers
Super-gainers	13%	4%	6%
Gainers	39%	30%	29%
Weight stable	33%	45%	42%
Weight losers	15%	21%	23%

Of particular interest is the fact that, contrary to popular belief, almost as many smokers (48%) either lost weight or remained stable, as those who gained weight (52%) after quitting smoking. Also, only around 17% more quitters than continuing smokers or non-smokers gained weight in that time, suggesting the problem is not just confined to smokers.

Comparisons between identical and non-identical twins showed that there was a greater equality of weight loss after quitting among the identical twins. This suggests a genetic factor may also be important in determining whether weight gain occurs after quitting smoking.

152. Don't get too comfortable after a meal

The thought of a tasty roast followed by port in front of the log fire is enough to get even the hardiest of dieters salivating. But while the roast and port might be passable—even for the weight conscious—a post-prandial (after-dinner) warming by the fire might add more to those calories gained during the meal than you realise.

This is the implication of a clever piece of research carried out recently in Sweden. Researchers tested heat loss following a meal in obese and normal weight people, some of the latter being kept warm by blankets and plastic coverings around the waist.

**A post-prandial
(after-dinner) warming by
the fire might add more to
those calories gained
during the meal than
you realise.**

Warm-wrapping the stomach following food intake in non-obese people resulted in reduced heat loss similar to that observed in the obese. Non-obese subjects who were not warm-wrapped lost more heat and therefore burned more energy than either of the other groups.

It's proposed that the reduced thermogenic (heat-producing) effect of food in obese people could be due to their extra 'padding', or warmth around the middle. The implication of this is that over-warming after a meal could be a disadvantage. The post-prandial port in front of the fire might be best avoided—but that's only if you're more serious about weight loss than about comfort.

153. Don't start if you don't think you can do it

Research from the Obesity Unit at the Royal Prince Alfred Hospital in Sydney has shown that women who score low on a measure of 'stages of change' and a measure of 'self-efficacy' are most likely to 'drop off the wagon' when it comes to maintaining a weight control lifestyle program. 'Stages of change' is a theory which predicts phases that people go through in any behaviour change. The five stages are:

1. pre-contemplation; 2. contemplation; 3. decision;
4. action; and 5. maintenance.

Women who haven't reached at least the 'decision' stage and who also have a low 'self-efficacy' or confidence about their chances of success on any program, tend to have a much greater rate of failure than those who had committed and really believed they could do it. The moral? Don't try until you're committed and you're sure you can do it.

154. Try a real fat farm—if you dare!

The classic 'fat farm'—where wealthy indulgers go to shed pounds, as well as dollars—sounds like a dream holiday. They're usually in ideal climates with comfortable surroundings, minimal food and rigorous exercise classes.

But as Melbourne dietitian Dr Matthew Fisher points out, these are the opposite conditions to those conditions shown scientifically to help metabolise fat. According to Dr Fisher, a proper 'fat farm' would:

- Be set in the snow to capitalise on the metabolic benefits of cold
- Involve moving around in the nude in the snow (for the same reason as above)
- Require physical activity (in the nude, in the snow) before breakfast—to capitalise on the extra fat burning which occurs after a night-time fast
- Include injections of prolactin, the female hormone associated with breastfeeding, to mobilise body fat
- Include apples and oranges as snack foods to accompany alcohol
- Have small spicy meals every four hours
- Make coffee consumption mandatory—at least up to four cups a day
- Insist on extended breastfeeding (for women) to maintain the high energy use of lactation
- Have no après-meal *gluweins* by the fire

It all makes more sense physiologically than the current version of the 'fat farm'. Still, it could be a little hard to sell to the average punter.

155. Use the best behavioural techniques

Modern psychological practice has shown the best techniques for long-term weight loss. According to Professor John Foreyt from Baylor College, Texas, evidence from all the behavioural research currently available suggests that greatest success in weight control programs will come from the following 8 points:

1. Attempting to change negative feelings, particularly depression and anxiety
2. Focusing on the pressure of social situations such as travelling and entertaining.
3. Having clients self-monitor their behaviours
4. Increasing internal motivation
5. Developing a network of social support
6. Carrying out regular physical activity
7. Setting goals at very gradual, rather than large, sudden changes
8. Setting realistic goals

7

WEIGHT-LOSS PRODUCTS AND PROGRAMS: THE GOOD, THE BAD AND THE UGLY

Everyone who's overweight wants a magic pill. They'd like to take it at night, so they can wake up in the morning and be trim, taut and terrific. Unfortunately, it's not as easy as that. Extra fat, like extra money, takes a long time to accumulate. Unlike extra money though, it also takes a long time to spend.

In the meantime, there are lots of shady dealers out there who'll try to convince you that if you spend your extra money with them, they'll spend your extra fat at the same rate. New products and programs for weight loss spring up faster than mushrooms after a rainstorm. Most will disappear as quickly as they surface, although in the meantime their backers will have quietly pocketed your extra wallet fat and moved on to the next fad.

Of course, not all new products or programs are bad. The move to low-fat foods, the development of new exercise machines and controlled behaviour modification programs, for example, all can have benefits (although none should be seen as 'magic'). We've labelled a range of these under the heading 'THE GOOD'. On the other hand, there are products that either work against any effort you might make to keep your body weight down, or are likely to be neutral in effect. We've considered some of these under the heading 'THE BAD'. This doesn't mean they should be totally avoided, but just used in moderation and with knowledgeable care. Finally, there's what we call 'THE UGLY'. These are products with no acceptable scientific backing, sold with the sole purpose of making their marketers fat on the proceeds. Pick your way through 'the good', try to find your way around 'the bad', but don't let yourself be fooled by 'the ugly'. All, we might add, are considered from a base of no financial or any other remunerative connection with the current author.

THE GOOD

156. Low-fat Fruitfuls may hit the spot

Fruit biscuits might be expected to be just that i.e. fruit-full. And so they would be if it wasn't for the pastry used to make them a biscuit. Unfortunately, wheat flour already contains some oils and extra oil has to be added to the flour to make a workable dough. Food technologists at Arnott's Biscuits, however, have worked out a fermentation process optimising the activity of the yeast and lactobacilli which make up the microflora of a fermenting dough. By combining this with a yeast mix at the mixing stage, only a minimum of fat or vegetable oils needs to be added. This has formed the basis of a new fruit biscuit from Arnott's called 'Fruitfuls', which meets all the requirements for a low-fat (i.e. 3%) tasty snack. Fruit in the biscuit is also specially prepared with a unique process originally developed in New Zealand. It saves the biscuit from spoiling and increases the intensity of the taste.

157. Undressing salad dressings

Usually made on an oil base, salad dressings normally repre-
sent an energy-dense way of topping a normally low-energy
salad. Some manufacturers are now providing an option with
vinegar-based dressings that taste fairly much like the real
thing. Both Kraft 'Free' and Kraft 'Light' have absolutely no
fat, as do the range of Praise' 'No Oil' salad dressings. Kraft
also provides less than 1% fat versions of the traditional
Thousand Island dressings. Salad Magic also has a range of
'no oil' dressings in the traditional national styles with less
than 1% fat, thus expanding the options for those who can't
yet take to undressing a salad.

158. The Ab machine: now this one may work

Machines for reducing fat on the stomach seem to come
and go with no real impact (see 'THE BAD' to follow). With
increasing education the public is becoming more aware
that fat is not reduced by spot reduction of the abdomen.
On the other hand, muscle tone and strength can be improved by trunk flexion (such as in sit-ups). A range of new
abdominal flex machines capitalise on a unique design which
isolates sit-up movements to the abdomen and provides a
comprehensive abdominal work-out. While the same applies
to fat loss as in any isolation exercise, these devices do
appear to actually work the abdomen and improve abdominal
musculature.

159. Another abdominal machine that might work

The Flexi-Tester is one of a myriad of abdominal development
products, most of which have disappeared from the scene.
But this one may be different. Based on tension from rubber
bands, the device involves flexing the trunk against the

resistance of a padded bar held against the upper ribs and stabilised between the legs. Sitting up against the device, or raising the legs to the trunk, guarantees the use of the abdominal muscles—if the exercise is carried out properly.

It should be remembered, however, that machines such as this (or other ab machines) in no way guarantee fat loss from the trunk, although they may improve abdominal muscle strength and tone. Fat is still only lost from the trunk region, like elsewhere, through aerobic activity. There may also be potential problems if lower back exercises aren't combined with the device to balance trunk strength.

160. Cod-liver oil: Granny may have been right after all

Oils *are* oils. Or so it's been thought. In fact all of them— mono, poly and saturated—are thought to have the same calorific value and therefore to make you fat to the same degree. But some very recent scientific research suggests there may just be something different in the oils that make up fish and most other different types of seafood. Whether it's the type, amount or other nutrients in fish that helps fat loss is not certain. But it seems that a good seafood diet (minus frying, batter or added oils) can help break through those fat-loss plateaus. Even the much maligned prawn may be due for a rebirth, and lobster (if you can afford it). Instead of Granny's cod-liver oil though, there may be more benefit in the whole cod. Tastes better too.

161. Thigh-splitting protection

It's one thing to try to be healthy by walking daily. It's another to cop blisters between the thunder-thighs for doing so. Rubbing thighs are a problem not often considered by the lean and healthy when they proselytise about exercise for the not-so-lean. But it's a reality. Fortunately, technology has an answer: the Lycra bike pant! Worn on their own, or underneath more conventional attire, Lycra pants reduce the effects of flesh on flesh, allowing the effort which helps decrease the cause of the problem—too much flesh!

162. Finding fibre as fat-free food

High-fibre biscuits (around 7 g of fibre a day) added to the weight control diet of a group of overweight Swedes at Karolinska Hospital in Stockholm over a twelve week period increased weight loss by an extra 2 kg on average. The extra food taken in as biscuits seemed to decrease the total volume of other food taken in over the rest of the day. Care needs to be taken when selecting high-fibre biscuits, however, that they're not also high in fat.

163. Olé for oleic

A new margarine-type spread from Flora includes oil from a new variety of sunflower specially modified to be high in mono-unsaturated oils, which are thought to be preventive in heart disease. The new sunflower breed is high in a form of oil called oleic acid which is more stable under heating than canola oil, the other most recently preferred mono-unsaturate. Flora Mono Sun margarine doesn't lose its taste as quickly as canola products because of a lower rate of oxidation and therefore deterioration. But while this new breed of sunflower oil is likely to now pervade all fat-based foods and perhaps decrease the risk of heart disease, it still needs to be pointed out that gram for gram it's still as fattening as all other forms of oil.

164. The low-fat ice cream war

If you love ice cream but don't like its long-term effects on your waistline, changes in ice cream technology may leave your mouth watering. New processes for reducing milk fats have led to a range of tasty new products on the market with names as tempting as 'Too Good to Be True'. New labelling laws allow ice creams with a fat content of from 3% (Peters) to 7% (Streets Blue Ribbon, Oak, etc.) to be sold as ice cream.

In most cases fat content has been dropped drastically (look for products with less than 10% fat—not 10% less fat!), with definite health advantages. For the waist watcher though, sugar content can also be a problem. And while 'energy per serving size' on labels will give an indication of this, check to make sure serving sizes are realistic. Will you really stop at a thimbleful in a serving?

165. A beer, my love, and . . .

What to have for 'nibblies' with a beer: that's a common refrain among waist-watching men. From products now on the market:

1. Parker's Pretzels: A low-fat (but reasonably high-salt) nibbly that provides taste, although not a lot of nutritional goodness.
2. Low-fat cracker-style biscuits: These include Ryvita and some versions of Vita-Weat (e.g. cracked pepper). Look for brands with less than 10 g of fat per 100 g.
3. Rice crackers: These may be high in salt, but because they're not cooked in oil, they are low in fat.
4. Low-fat popcorn: Home-popped corn (not smothered with butter) and some new varieties soon to be on the market are low in fat. Some even have added spices for an extra advantage. Beware of the commercially popped varieties and those which have been hot-buttered.
5. Low-fat cheeses: Most cheeses sold as 'low fat' are simply 'lower fat' than they were. Check that total fat content is less than 10%. Two reasonably tasty examples are Bega

Super Light and Devondale 7 (block cheese, not sand-wich slices).

6. Low-fat potato crisps: Crisps which are baked and up to 97% fat-free are set to hit the market in 1997 and are likely to have a major impact on other crisps on the market.

166. Rinsing meat patties to reduce fat . . .

For those with a taste for hamburgers, but a problem with cholesterol or calories—here's a new way of cooking to reduce both. In a study carried out at the University of Iowa scientists compared ground beef crumbles made with initial levels of 10%, 20% and 30% fat after they had been panfried, panbroiled or microwaved. After cooking, half of the crumbles were rinsed in warm water to remove fat.

Surprisingly, the effects of cooking methods on fat levels were quite small, the initial fat levels being the biggest indicator of fat levels after cooking. Rinsing with warm water after cooking, however, significantly reduced fat and increased the moisture content of the crumbles, while not causing any substantial losses in protein, iron, zinc or vitamin B12 levels. This technique therefore may be effective not only for those watching their waists, but also for those on low-fat, low-cholesterol diets.

167. . . . or 'lean linking' them . . .

If you're not up to rinsing your beef patties but still have a mind for a hamburger, Woolworths have come up with an alternative as part of their Lean Links low-fat range. Lean Links hamburger patties, made from reduced fat beef, contain around 7–8 grams of fat per patty (compared with around 30 grams in the average shop-bought hamburger). They come frozen in packs of four and a patty takes 4–5 minutes to thaw out and grill—an added bonus for the time-strapped executive. The only problem might be the temptation to eat more because of the reduced-fat and calorie content. Remember that these are low-fat, and not no-fat products.

168. . . . or going all the way

If low-fat *individual* products are not enough, the answer may be to go to low-fat whole meals—and to have these delivered, prepared and ready to heat. This is the thinking behind the meals from The Diet Factory and some other newer companies. These are healthy, low-fat, pre-prepared meals provided to dieters and busy executives throughout Australia. Meals are delivered to the doorstep for as many days or weeks as desired with the average cost of a week's meals around what it would cost someone to feed themselves. These meals are not meant to eliminate thinking by dieters, but rather to provide examples of the type of healthy food that can help reduce fat.

169. The benefits of yoga

The practice of yoga is known to often aid weight loss. Yet exercise scientists claim that the amount of effort required in yoga is not enough to gain the weight-loss benefits of exercise. An alternative explanation has been that yoga reduces the stress which causes the over-eating that results in obesity. Indian researchers, however, have found that yoga increases the body's metabolic rate by up to 20%, and it may be this which has the long-term effects on weight loss. The reason could be the forced expiration of air that's practiced in some forms of yoga.

170. Thin fish

Fried fish fillets are usually a no-no for waist watchers. But food technologists at Bird's Eye have managed to reduce the fat and salt content of their Lite 'n Healthy fish fillets by eliminating the pre-cooking process, which means that the fillets are only cooked once—at home—and so don't absorb as much oil. With a healthier mix of cooking oils, including mono-unsaturated canola oil rather than saturated animal fats in the mixture, the product now has not only less fat, but a healthier mixture of fats. But you still have to consider the total fat.

171. Lamb on the trim

Trim Lamb is part of the Australian Meat and Livestock Corporation's latest campaign to capture the consumer mood for low-fat, low-calorie convenience in food. It's designed to promote new low-fat boneless cuts of lamb. Trim Lamb *is* lower in fat and hence calories and should be a preferred substitute for those who like meat but want to lose weight. It could also compete with other low-fat meats and chicken in cholesterol management.

172. New cheeses on the whey

Like much of what's nice, cheese is fattening and a high source of cholesterol. With other dairy products, like milk, cream or yoghurt, it's been relatively simple to reduce the fat content and keep the flavour. Cheese has been more difficult, and the early methods resulted in a bland-tasting product.

Now food technologists have made a tasty cheese with 7–10% fat (compared to 35% in traditional cheeses) which is suitable for weight and cholesterol watchers. New brands available include Bega Super Light and Devondale 7 (currently available only from delicatessens). More are expected in the future.

173. Popcorn or potato crisps?

The battle for the low-fat nibbly is on. Among the protagonists: popcorn v potato crisps. But the fight is decidely uneven. Figures produced by the University of California (Berkeley) Wellness Letter suggest that you would have to eat nearly 400 grams of plain, unbuttered popcorn to get the calories available in 25 grams of potato crisps (about 15 crisps). By substituting one cup of plain, unbuttered popcorn for a 25 gram bag of potato crisps you save around 130 calories and 10 grams of fat.

174. Biscuits you can eat

One of the biggest problems for anyone watching their fat intake is snack foods. Most are high in fats and oils and substitutes are often difficult to make. The following is a list of biscuits which contain fat levels below 10%, as suggested on the GutBuster program.

	fat %		fat %
Arnott's		**Crackerbread**	
Fruitfuls	3.0	Toasted Crispbread	2.9
Salada Multi-grain	8.7	Wholewheat & rye	3.0
Vita-Weat Cracked Pepper	8.8	**Sunfarm**	
Cracked Pepper Water Crackers	8.4	Rice Cakes	2.5
Cruskits	2.5		
Rye Cruskits	low		
Ryvita			
Original	2.5		
Cracked Pepper	3.3		
Golden Rye	2.5		

175. The low-fat DIY potato crisper

Perhaps the best snack with a beer is potato crisps. But crisps are usually extremely high in fat (around 38%)

because of the large surface area which soaks up the oil in which they're cooked. If you can get rid of the oil, the fat content and fat consequences are eliminated.

Enter the no-fat-do-it-yourself microwave potato chip maker. Available from mail order suppliers for the blinding fee of $9.95, the chip maker is a simple microwaveable plastic device in which chips sliced from any type of potato are stood upright. The microwaving technique allows the water to be reduced from the potato while it is being cooked, without the need for oil. Thy're crunchy and tasty.

176. Drugs—a second generation

Medications for obesity have had an undistinguished track record. Initially based on stimulants such as the amphetamines, their effect was usually short-lived with the potential for addiction and a sudden regain of weight on cessation. More recently, however, a second generation of medications has been developed which have an effect on the chemical neuro-transmitters in the brain associated with hunger. The two main versions of this serotonin facilitator, D-fenfluramine (Adifax, Redux) and sibutramine (Reductil), have their effect through reduced food intake, but are non-addictive and therefore appear to be able to be taken for longer with few side effects. Despite their effectiveness, the medications still require an asssociated lifestyle program of eating and exercise to be truly effective. They're also recommended only for those who have had no success with lifestyle programs alone.

A possible third generation of even more effective drugs may arise from current complex microbiological research on obesity, including the potential discovery of gene products and molecular manipulation of natural chemicals such as growth hormone. Derivatives of these medications are likely to become available around the turn of the century.

THE BAD

177. Chipping away at crisps

Potato crisp manufacturers have tried to jump on the health bandwagon through the introduction of 'light' and 'lightly salted' varieties. Some of these, such as the 'Kettle chip', were criticised by nutritionists for their use of saturated fats such as palm oils, which are thought to increase cholesterol levels in the bloodstream. But manufacturers have been quick to counter, using claims such as 'no cholesterol' and 'no tropical oils'. The argument seems to have been taken away from the issue of energy intake which, considering a standard snack-sized bag contains around 700 calories and 38 g of fat, is probably more of an issue for many consumers.

178. Some thin attempts to hide fat crisps

Crisps are one of the fattier ways of treating potatoes. With public awareness of fat content increasing, crisp manufacturers are trying all kinds of tricks to disguise this fact. Among the new techniques:

- Use a name that implies low-fat without ever being so: This is the method behind Thins, also promoted as 'cholesterol free', but which contain 31.4% fat, and Smith's Lites, which are actually only lightly salted, but have a fat content of 33.5%.
- Use a healthy sounding crisp base: Vege chips not only have the healthy sound of a vegetable ingredient (although potato is also a vegetable), they are promoted as 'all natural ingredients' and 'cholesterol free'. They still have over 20% fat. Soya King Multigrain Crisps, playing on the healthful qualities of soy beans, have 27.4% fat.

179. Peanut butter—off the list

Peanuts, in most forms, are high in oil. Peanut butter mixes range between 30–60% fat. Even if this is spread lightly on bread or toast, it can amount to 5–6 grams per slice. At least half of this then is fat. Being used on top of butter, which it usually is, adds another 3–4 grams of fat. Probably more important is the more-ishness of peanut butter as a food, similar to that craving for 'just another handful' of peanuts when they are eaten on their own. While by no means junk food, peanut butter is not the spread for those wishing to avoid the spread.

180. Farmed seafood—is it the same?

With the oceans' natural resources being taxed to the limits, there is an increasing move towards farming seafood—prawns, trout, even the fast moving tuna are now being kept in relatively confined ocean pens in some parts of southern Australia.

But does the quality of the seafood stay the same? Or do fish and prawns, like cattle and chicken that are confined, change their type and amount of fat and therefore their health benefits for those higher up the food chain, i.e. us?

This question is being looked at seriously by marine food scientists throughout the world. So far there are no definite answers, although it is apparent that fat types and levels are dependent on the type of food eaten and amount of energy expended by the animal.

In one study carried out on rainbow trout in the United Kingdom, both fat composition and immune system products differed in fish fed a more natural organic diet compared with those fed a sunflower-oil compound. It's not yet clear what effects this would have on the human consumer.

In the meantime, it's known that eating ocean-bred or 'wild' seafood does have health and possibly even fat-loss benefits. The type of fatty acids in fish (called EPA for eicosapentaenoic acid) have been shown to decrease human cholesterol levels. Studies are also now being done to assess their effects in body weight maintenance, with some suggestion that it may not just be the amount but also the type of fats that are beneficial for the waist watcher.

Aquaculture is undoubtedly the way of the future. It remains to be seen whether it will have any of the negative effects on health and fatness that have come from other forms of farming.

181. Let them (not) eat cake

What is it that turns the average lean machine into a fat pack? Too much cake, biscuits and chocolates, you may well think. After all, it's these that stand out in any list of no-nos for getting rid of that spare tyre.

However, researchers at Leeds University's Biopsychology Group, who've made a specialty of studying human tastes, food preferences and fat patterns, don't think this is the answer. From analysing food intake patterns of groups of fat and lean people, they've found that the former do indeed eat more foods that are higher in fat, including more meat, fried potatoes, nuts, butter, eggs and cheese. But fat people also eat less carbohydrate-rich foods like fruit, vegetables, breakfast cereal, skimmed milk or rice and pasta. The occasional chocolate treat (if you can stop at one) perhaps shouldn't rate on the guilt index—at least if the bigger items are taken care of.

182. 'Natural' fruit juices

The term 'natural' is often used as a marketing tool—as if manufacturers are doing us a favour by allowing food to remain in its normal state. Yet 'natural' doesn't always imply 'better', particularly when it comes to high-energy foods.

And so it is with fruit juices. Most are plenty sweet enough and never needed the benefits of 'no added sugar'. But because they're high in concentrated natural sugars (with most fibre removed), they're also high in energy. Their value in other vitamins and minerals doesn't compensate for the weight-gaining effects of the drink—'natural' or not.

'Natural' doesn't always imply 'better', particularly when it comes to high-energy foods.

183. 'Light' what?

Changes to food labelling regulations in Australian will soon see the elimination of a practice that has confused the weight-conscious food buyer for some time. Manufacturers will be required to be more specific on foods labelled 'light' or 'lite'. The confusion has been in being able to add the labels to foods that are reduced in just about anything— sugar, salt, fat, calories (even colour, in the case of olive oil). Yet the term 'light' implies 'low in energy' and therefore not fattening.

184. Fruit juicers: are they necessary?

Fruit juicers have become a modern 'diet' tool promoted for their health benefits—fruit juices are high in vitamins and minerals. But are they really necessary?

Most juicers work by extracting high fibre pulp from fluid. This is the first process where value is lost. Fibre is an important part of the diet and one of the major reasons for the recommendations for increased fruit and vegetable input in the diet.

Some juice machines liquify the entire fruit or vegetable,

thus retaining some fibre. But this results in a thick mushy juice that requires diluting with water before drinking. When the mix is diluted, the concentration of vitamins is thus altered, reducing the value per volume of fluid. Hence, while whole fruit is wholesome, low fat and recommended, you can save your money on the fruit juicer.

185. The downside of fruit juice

Because it takes around 500 g of fruit to make a cup of fruit juice, the sugar (and therefore energy) value of the juice becomes highly concentrated. On the other hand it's very easy to drink a cup of fruit juice, while it would be quite filling to eat the whole fruit which made it up. Fruit juice therefore is quite fattening, relative to the quantity of whole fruit from which it's made.

JUICE MYTHS

- Fresh juice is more nutritious than processed juices. **False**. As long as processed juices are handled properly they retain the value of fresh juices.
- Juice is as good as the whole fruit. **False**. Fruit contains more than just juice (particularly fibre), which adds to its value.
- Juice is not fattening. **False**. Because juice represents concentrated sugar (without the benefit of fibre), it can be as fattening as the sugar in normal soft drink.
- Commercial juicers are better than hand squeezing. **False**. They may make the job easier, but because most juicers eliminate fibre they are probably less healthy than the hand squeezed variety.
- Juice is better than milk for infants. **False**. Although some juice may be desirable, a high level of energy intake from fruit juice can mean infants miss out on other vital nutrients in the diet.

WHAT ABOUT VEGETABLE JUICES?

Because vegetables are generally lower in sugars than fruit, most vegetable juices are lower in total energy than fruit juices. Homemade vegetable juices contain roughly the same calories as the vegetable itself and can generally be consumed quite liberally without excessive weight gain.

Fruit juice can also increase blood triglyceride levels, thereby increasing disease risks in susceptible people. For this reason the overweight should be particularly cautious about high intakes of fruit juices, just as much as the underweight might be cautious about the risks of becoming overweight.

The rise in blood sugars caused by drinking fruit juice can also be a disadvantage in those with diabetes, or with undetected diabetic tendencies. Blood sugar increases after drinking fruit juice are little different to those from drinking the same amount of regular soft drink. Whole fruit causes a less rapid rise in blood sugar than fruit juice.

For those with a weight problem, fruit juice should be avoided in favour of the whole fruit. Fruit juice has no extraordinary health benefits, although in the normal weight healthy individual it can provide an important source of energy and nutrients.

186. Butter, margarine or . . . ?

The butter–margarine squabble has been around for years. And it's not likely to be resolved in the near future because of new findings continually being presented by both camps: butter is more natural, margarine is lower in saturated fat; butter is more stable, margarine can be produced from healthy mono-unsaturated oils. On a health basis, the solution is unclear. In terms of weight control, however, there's little dispute: both butter and margarine are high in fats and oils, which contain 9 cal/g—irrespective of type—and so have a similar effect on body fat gain. Only a teaspoonful of either will yield around 35 kcal—hence the rush by food technologists to come up with a lower-fat, or no-fat, alternative spread. Until they do, the answer seems to be to use neither—or spread as thinly as possible—for the serious waist watcher.

> **Both butter and margarine**
> **are high in fats and oils,**
> **which contain**
> **9 cal/g—irrespective of**
> **type—and so have a similar**
> **effect on body fat gain.**

187. The new sugar-lite, but fat-heavy, chocolate

Climbing on the 'lite' bandwagon, one major chocolate manufacturer has produced a 'lite' chocolate by substituting artificial sweetener for the more calorie-dense 'natural' sugars that make up a significant component of the calories in chocolate.

While this does indeed reduce the energy content and make a chocolate lower in calories that the sugared version, the main energy problem remains. Chocolate contains significant amounts of saturated fat. Fat is more energy dense than sugar (9 calories per gram compared to 4.5 calories per gram) and more potentially atherogenic (i.e. causing blocking of the arteries through build up of fats such as cholesterol).

'Lite' chocolate may indeed therefore be 'liter' than non 'lite' chocolate. But it's still hardly a diet food, as the name implies to many.

188. Soft drink might be as much a cause of a beer gut as beer

Lack of exercise and eating too much are always blamed as the main causes of overweight. But an often unrecognised contributor to the fat stakes is soft drinks.

Retail World magazine in 1994 published a survey showing that three of the ten biggest selling items in supermarkets are soft drinks—with Coca-Cola by far the most popular. Despite our increasing interest in health, diet drinks still lag well behind.

Research with the overweight, particularly men, has shown that many aren't aware that soft drinks can be as fattening as beer. Food analysis charts (see box) indicate differently. Soft drink manufacturers worldwide are becoming increasingly sensitive to the role they are seen to play in promoting obesity. With some people now never drinking any other type of liquid, the industry has cause for concern at its image.

The rush is also on for alternative low-calorie sweeteners with a better taste than the current variety. This is also

ENERGY CONTENT OF VARIOUS DRINKS (CALORIES)

Low alcohol beer	285 mL (10 oz) middy	70
Regular beer	285 mL middy	105
Stout	285 mL middy	160
Table wine	125 mL (4 oz) glass	85
Fortified wine	60 mL (2 oz) glass	80
1 nip spirits	30 mL (1 oz) (with nothing added except water or soda)	60
Orange juice	250 mL glass	90
Cola (sugared)	370 mL can	160
Orange-flavoured soft drink	370 mL can	200

likely to prove a highly profitable industry in the future. Meanwhile, those with a weight problem might be better advised to break the soft drink habit than to go on low-calorie food binges.

189. 'Vegarine' or 'Buttamite'?

Vegemite is a great Australian food. As the ads tell us, it's choc-full of vitamins (B in particular), low in fat and designed to make us happy, energetic and, by implication, healthy. Nothing wrong with this. In fact, nothing wrong with the product *per se*.

But like all goody goodies, Vegemite is tainted by the company it keeps. As you've no doubt noticed, it's difficult to eat vegemite on bread or toast without some kind of spread—usually butter or margarine—even if you are Australian! Spreads, of course, are amongst the highest fat foods, and hence most fattening, on the market—up to 80% fats or oils for both butter and margarine.

Unfortunately, Vegemite screams out for a fatty partner, so much so that it has now been added in to some cheese products. In truth, it may have been better to mix in the butter or margarine in the first place and call it 'Vegarine' or 'Buttamite'. Unless you can learn to live with it without a spread (or with very little) it may work counter to what you're trying to do with your waistline.

190. If you're thinking about liposuction, be prepared for the fat to come back

The after-effects of liposuction (removing fat cells from body parts with suction) or lipectomy (cutting off fat cells) have never really been documented. It's thought that re-growth of fat cells might occur naturally. Now there's a suggestion from work with animals that surgical removal of fat might cause abnormalities in blood fats like triglyceride and cholesterol. There's also an indication that this may be one time when fat cells can regenerate, making the outcome of the process negligible.

191. Glasses, seaweed and all of the below

The range of gimmicks that have been promoted for weight loss at some stage or other is almost too numerous (and often too ridiculous) to mention. But among those you can immediately cross off your list are:

- Dark glasses that make food look less appealing
- Seaweed
- Weight-loss soap
- Acupressure ear pins
- Vibrating belts
- Vibrating roller machines
- The 'xxx' diet (substitute your own term).

Three basic principles are necessary (but not necessarily sufficient) for recognising weight control myths. The first, related to exercise, is:

> *'If you don't work, it doesn't work.'*

The second, related to nutrition, suggests that:

> *'Any food that reduces total energy input can decrease weight—temporarily!'*

Both are qualified by the third principle which states:

> *'If you can't imagine doing this for the rest of your life, it won't work.'*

192. Holding off Olestra

The non-digestible fat-based fat substitute Olestra, produced by American food giant Proctor and Gamble, was approved by the US Food and Drug Administration for general consumption in January 1996. Its release has given cause for concern among nutritionists worried about what we don't know about the product. Here are some facts:

- *What is it?* Olestra is a glucose polyester manufactured by combining a sugar with fat molecules from vegetable fats.
- *How does it work?* Most fats consist of three fatty acids plus a molecule of glycerol (triglycerides) which are then 'split apart' by enzymes in the gut to be digested. Olestra consists of six fatty acids hung together by a molecule of sucrose which is too big and densely packed to be enzymatically split and digested. It therefore passes through the body unabsorbed.
- *What are its uses?* Because Olestra is fat based, it has the 'mouth feel' of ordinary fat. Unlike other non-fat based substitutes, it is also stable in cooking and frying and therefore can come as a cooking oil as well as food additive.
- *What are its advantages?* It adds no calories, is tasty like fat, has been shown to reduce blood cholesterol and can be used in cooking.
- *What are its disadvantages?* It may 'drain' certain vitamins and minerals, may have an effect on bowel habits, may cause 'anal leakage' and has an 'aftertaste' not present with fat. Other long-term health effects are not known.
- *What is the solution?* If blood fats or obesity are the problem, low-fat or no-fat foods are the first preference. If this is hard to maintain, fat substitutes like Olestra *may* be the next alternative. However, these should be taken in moderation, at least until long-term safety benefits have been established. Its release by authorities in the United States against the wishes of many qualified specialists is a signal for caution.

THE UGLY

193. Fat-burning tablets to burn

Fat metabolisers or 'mobilisers' are touted in health food stores and gymnasiums as the latest in fat-reducing agents. These are advertised with a range of promises, such as 'converts fat to fuel' or 'improves muscle definition'. However, a review by respected National Heart Foundation nutritionists Glen Cardwell and Nicole Fruin poors cold water on any fat-burning fire.

Products currently promoted have as common ingredients carnitine, inositol and choline, and sometimes various vitamins, lecithin and herbs. They are generally aimed at the sports market, but with sales through pharmacies often to those desperate to try anything. According to Cardwell and Fruin there is no scientific backing for any of the claims made by any of the products. Even if they did 'mobilise' fat, they point out, fat must still be burned up through exercise: 'it doesn't evaporate from the body'.

194. Skin patches—the latest in shonky dealings

We've been there before: special 'magic' ingredients that melt away fat by the hour. This time though, the technique is different. All you have to do is attach a skin patch to the body (like wearing a Band-Aid) and you can 'dissolve your fat cells by the hour'.

Selling under the name of Medex Diet Patch or Slender Patch (obviously two different agents), the diet patches have the ring of *déjà vu* about them. The 'magic ingredient' is a substance called *focus vesiculosis* which (surprise, surprise) comes from North Sea seaweeds (which just happen to be inaccessible to the average person). The seaweed trick has been tried several times before but the advent of the slowly absorbed medical patch (like the nicotine patch for smokers) has given a whole new life to the product.

Of interest (despite claims that all the best medical journals have raved about it) is our failure to find any reports on the substance in reputable medical journals, or any research reported at recent International Obesity conferences. On top of this, recent reports suggest that weight loss of greater than 1.5 kg/week could be a health risk, yet diet patch sellers claim a loss of 2 kg/week—'even if you are a big eater'. Avoid getting stuck on this one!

195. Ear pressure: another way of getting 'clipped'?

Ear clips are yet another of the myriad promises currently doing the rounds for fat loss. These are based on providing

"DAMMIT FIONA, I SAID A RICH DOCTOR"

'acupuncture without needles', otherwise known as acupressure. Different products are available, all needing to be worn on the ear before and after meals. Through a complex process (generally explained half in Chinese medical terms and half in English terms) this is supposed to reduce the appetite and 'tell the brain that the stomach is full'.

Ear clips have been comprehensively trounced by the US Federal Trade Commission, largely on the basis of the claims made for them. In particular, there is no evidence that they reduce hunger, cause weight or fat loss, or control food intake. More tellingly, a controlled study of acupressure and its effects on weight loss many years ago (*American Journal of Clinical Nutrition*, 1976:29:832–835) showed absolutely no effect in weight loss. On top of this, there is no guarantee that the available products really do perform acupressure. You're likely to do just as well wearing ordinary earrings.

196. Brindleberry: your time is up

What do you do with a 'fat-burning' product when the explanation for its effects is pulled out from under it? Brindleberry, a 'natural' fat-loss product, is an example. Brindleberry products are marketed in health food shops as preventing the conversion of carbohydrate to fat through the mystical sounding chemical ATP-citrate amylase. Now a number of scientific studies as well as general scientific opinion indicate that conversion of fat from carbohydrate— *de novo* lipogenesis is the technical term—does not occur under normal physiological circumstances in humans. Only fat in foods is readily stored as fat in the body. Brindleberry sellers do have a reserve ace up their sleeves though. The product, they say, also reduces hunger. It's always good to have an unrelated explanation in case of the unexpected!

197. Slim Fit: the 'slim' is in the shorts, not in you

Having (almost) given up on fad treatments for weight loss, some marketers are now turning to ways to at least hide what you've got. Waist Away is an 'instant waist trimmer', sold through mail order catalogues, that acts like a belly corset to pull the waist in. It only has a cosmetic effect and the marketers are smart enough to say so. Slim Fit, which are tight long-length shorts for women, on the other hand claim to have a direct effect on fat loss. Advertising suggests that the product 'uses heat and micro massage to promote the removal of waste and draws superfluous fat and water molecules from the skin's surface'—a physiological impossibility which must have been missed by advertising regulators. Wallet size is about the only thing that will be slimmed here.

198. Digital Tummy Trimmer: watch your dollars tick away

Yet another of the 'no effort', 'no push up' devices, the Digital Tummy Trimmer is a clever device that requires you to expand the stomach muscles against the pressure of a tight belt. The type of exercise required is isometric, or a contraction of muscles without movement. And while isometric actions have been shown to improve strength under certain conditions, and at the muscle length at which it is carried out, it is fallacious to say, as the marketers of this product do, that it will 'firm and flatten' your tummy.

199. Tummy trimmers—just wallet lighteners?

Despite countless warnings, they still keep coming—no-effort exercise machines to reduce stomach size. Sold under the promise of 'a flat stomach without sit-ups or exercise', they come in all forms, the latest being a pressurised vibration system advertised as being 'so easy to use, with absolutely no exercise'.

As with most previous claims, this flouts all known laws of exercise physiology. Although some methods may help tighten stomach muscles in certain circumstances (although not when there is no effort involved), it does little for overlying fat. This is only reduced by burning energy through aerobic exercise.

You could hardly therefore expect to get a flat stomach from any of these approaches. Yet as consumer affairs departments seem reluctant to act against the promotion of such devices without specific complaint, it's left to the principle of *caveat emptor*—'buyer beware'; in this case of all those who come bearing magical no-effort goods.

200. Don't come the magic prawn with me!

Promoters of weight-loss gimmicks have learned one thing in recent times: to sell the most of an unproven product you need to do it quickly. And to sell lots of product quickly, you needs lots of distributors with a multi-level marketing format.

The latest players in the market have a slightly different version of an old standby. Chitosan is a fibre supplement made from the shells of molluscs. It's sold in tablet form as a meal supplement, with the claim that it 'attracts' fats in the digestive tract and prevents them from being absorbed.

In the first place, there is no convincing evidence that this happens, nor that it can happen with supplement tablets such as prescribed. Secondly, if it does prevent absorption of fats, it would prevent absorption of good fats (omega-three, omega-six and linoleic acid) as well as bad fats, and fat-soluble vitamins such as vitamin E and beta carotene.

Beta carotene and some other products of the fat-soluble vitamin A are thought to be vital anti-cancer agents and malabsorption of any or all of these substances could be potentially dangerous.

Other similarities of the Chitosan story to standard weight-loss marketing gimmicks are:

- Claims of extensive scientific research supporting the product. On closer inspection, this mostly comes from obscure foreign language journals. The English language publications do not directly research the product or the supplements advocated.

- Proposals for a 'new', 'magic', 'amazing' discovery. The product, a form of fibre, is a variation on a theme. It just happens that it can't be easily grown in your backyard or bought at the corner store in the form of mollusc shells.

- False claims based on minimal research information: the fact that one rat study has shown a decrease in cholesterol with Chitosan does not indicate that it reduces fat in the diet. Many other mono- and poly-unsaturated oils reduce cholesterol, but this only happens after they are absorbed into the bloodstream.

- Aggressive marketing by unknowledgeable distributors: as a multi-level style marketing operation the product can be sold by anyone greedy enough to want a share of the action, without any knowledge of the potential dangers of the product.

- The implication that there is no need to otherwise control food intake: any supplement taken in the absence of a balanced eating plan poses potential health risks, independent of any possible long-term risks from the supplement itself.

Chitosan is not the first, nor will it be the last, weight control gimmick of its kind. The nature of its promotion, however, makes it categorisable in this section under the ugly category.

201. Body wraps—you might as well wrap the therapist in your $100 notes

They claim that it's been used for centuries: wrapping of the body in bandages and using 'secret' oils which increase the metabolism and 'instantly' decrease fat. The fact that this is neither physiologically feasible nor possible doesn't seem to matter. Centres selling the treatment appear to be doing a roaring trade. So, what can be wrong with it?

Wrapping causes sweating; sweat, being water, is heavy. After any length of time in a wrap, sweating, plus compression of the body cells, will give the impression of a loss of body weight and size. Naturally this is temporary. If the treatment does happen to work over the longer term it is simply because of the low-energy diet and exercise program prescribed with it.

If the 'magic' oil in the treatment worked as it is reputed to, it could only do so by penetrating the skin and causing a change in the body's metabolism. If this actually happened, the treatment would have to be scheduled under the prescribed drugs act. Either way, the so-called proof is non-existent. There is no respected scientific verification of this treatment. Anyone believing it should be wrapped up for life.

REFERENCES

Introduction: Egger G. and Swinburne B. *The Fat Loss Leader's Handbook*. Sydney, Allen & Unwin, 1996

1. Keys A. and others. *The Biology of Human Starvation*, School of Public Health. Minneapolis, University of Minnesota Press, 1950
2. Cardwell G. *Diet Addiction*, Wellness Australia, PO Box 519, Subiaco WA 6914
3. Shetty P.S. and others. 'Energy requirements of adults: An update on basal metabolic rates (BMRs) and physical activity levels (PALs).' *European Journal of Clinical Nutrition*, 1996: 50 (Suppl 1):S11–23
4. Larson D.E., Rising R., Ferraro R.T., Ravussin E. 'Spontaneous overfeeding with a "cafeteria diet" in men: effects on 24-hour energy expenditure and substrate oxidation.' *International Journal of Obesity*, 1995: 19:331–7
5. Raben A. and others. 'Spontaneous weight loss during 11 weeks' ad libitum intake of a low fat/high fibre diet

in young, normal weight subjects.' *International Journal of Obesity*, 1995: 19:916–23

6. St Joer E.R. and others. 'How eating patterns may relate to obesity.' *International Journal of Obesity*, 1995: (2):28

7. LeBlanc J. and others. 'Components of postprandial thermogenesis in relation to meal frequency in humans.' *Canadian Journal of Physiology and Pharmacology*, 1993: 71(12):879–83

8. Miller M.R. and Kose B. 'What are Western Australians Eating? The Perth Dietary Surveys.' Paper presented at the Nutrition WA Conference, 1996 (March 29).

9. Kristal A.R. and others. 'Patterns of dietary behaviour associated with selecting diets low in fat: Reliability and validity of a behavioural approach to dietary assessment.' *Journal of the American Dietetic Association*, 1990: 214–20

10. Matters R.D. 'Fat preference and adherence to a reduced-fat diet.' *American Journal of Clinical Nutrition*, 1993: 57:373–81

11. Siscovick D.S. and others. 'Dietary intake and cell membrane levels of long-chain n–3 polyunsaturated fatty acids and the risk of primary cardiac arrest.' *Journal of the American Medical Association*, 1995: 274:1363–7

12. Rolland-Cachera M.F., Deheeger M., Bellisle F. 'Early nutrition and later outcomes.' *International Journal of Obesity*, 1995: 19(2):11

13. Stanton R. *The Diet Dilemma*. Sydney, Allen & Unwin, 1991.

14. Blundell J. 'Food intake and appetite control: from energy intake to dietary patterns.' *International Journal of Obesity*, 1995: 19(2):1001–2

15. Holt S.H.A. and others. 'A satiety index of common foods.' *European Journal of Clinical Nutrition*, 1995: 49:675–90

16. Poppit, S.D. 'Energy density of diets and obesity.' *International Journal of Obesity*, 1995: 19 Supp 5:S20–6

17. Brand Miller J., Forster-Powell K. and Colaguri S. *The GI Factor*, Hodder & Stoughton, Sydney, 1996

18. Stephens A. 'More carbohydrates. Better health.' Paper presented to the International Life Sciences Conference on Carbohydrates and Health, Sydney, June, 1995; Tagliabue A. and others. 'The effect of raw potato starch on energy expenditure and substrate oxidation.' *American Journal of Clinical Nutrition*, 1995: 61:1070–5

19. Baghurst K. and others. 'The development of a simple dietary assessment and education tool.' *Journal of Nutrition Education*, 1992: 24:165–72.

20. Stanton R. *Food for Health*. Sydney, Allen & Unwin, 1989

21. Turconi G. and others. 'High-calorie fibre-rich breakfast: its effect on satiety.' *Journal of Human Nutrition & Dietetics*, 1993: 6:245–52

22. Stanton R. *The Diet Dilemma*. Sydney, Allen & Unwin, 1991.

23. Mela D.J. 'Consumer estimates of the energy from fat in common foods.' *European Journal of Clinical Nutrition*, 1993: 47:735–40

24. Egger G. and Stanton R. *The GutBuster 'Waist Loss Guide' for men*. Sydney, Allen & Unwin, 1993; Stanton R. *Eating for Peak Performance*. Sydney, Allen & Unwin, 1994

25. Emmett P.M. and Heaton K.W. 'Is extrinsic sugar a vehicle for dietary fat?' *Lancet*, 1995: 345:1537–40

26. Shied D.J. and Rolls B. 'Information about the fat content of preloads influences energy intake in healthy women.' *Journal of the American Dietetic Association*, 1995: 95:993–8

27. Ballard-Barbash R. and others. 'Variability in percent energy from fat throughout the day: Implications for application of total diet goals.' *Journal of Nutrition Education*, 1994: 26(6):278–83

28. Stanton R. 'Dietary extremism and eating disorders in athletes.' In *Clinical Sports Nutrition*, Burke L. and Deakin V. (eds), McGraw-Hill, Sydney, 1994

29. Radimer K.L. 'Assessment of magazine weight reduction diets for consistency with dietary guidelines and targets.' *Australian Journal of Nutrition and Dietetics*, 1995: 52(1):16–23

30. Drewnowski A. 'Intense sweeteners and the control of appetite.' *Nutrition Reviews*, 1995: 53(1):1–7

31. Waterhouse D. *Why women like chocolate*. New York, Vermilion Press, 1995; Drewnowski A. 'Food preferences in human obesity: carbohydrates versus fats.' *Appetite*, 1992: 18:207–21

32. Heitmann B.L. and Lissner L. 'Dietary under-reporting by obese individuals—is it specific or non-specific?' *British Medical Journal*, 1995: 311:986–9.

33. Colquhoun E.O. 'Possible new pharmacological approaches to the management of obesity.' Second Scientific Meeting of the Australian Society for the Study of Obesity, Melbourne, July 1993

34. Westerterp K. 'Diet induced thermogenesis and cumulative food intake curves as a function of familiarity with food and dietary restraint in humans.' *Physiology and Behaviour*, 1992: 5113:457–65

35. Bracco D. and others. 'Effects of caffeine on energy metabolism, heart rate, and methylxanthine metabolism in lean and obese women.' *American Journal of Physiology*, 1995: 269:E671–8

36. Pudel V. 'Psychological aspects of obesity.' In Cottrell R. (ed). *Weight control: the current perspective*, London, Chapman and Hall, 1995

37. Egger G. and Mowbray G. 'A qualitative analysis of obesity and at-risk overweight in working men.' *Australian Journal of Nutrition and Dietetics*, 1993: 50(1):10–14

38. Rumpler W.V. and others. 'Energy value of moderate

alcohol consumption by humans.' *American Journal of Clinical Nutrition*, 1996: 64:108–14

39. Cotton J.R. and others. 'Replacement of dietary fat with sucrose polyester: effects on energy intake and appetite control in nonobese males.' *American Journal of Clinical Nutrition*, 1996; 63:891–6

40. Gershoff S.N. 'Nutrition evaluation of dietary fat substitutes.' *Nutrition Reviews*, 1995: 53(11):305–13

41. Whitehead J.M., McNeill G. and Smith J.S. 'The effect of protein intake on 24-hour energy expenditure during energy restriction.' *International Journal of Obesity*, 1996: 20:727–32

42. NSW Health Department Report. 'Tips on Chips'. Sydney, 1996

43. Shetty P.S. and others. 'Energy requirements of adults: An update on basal metabolic rates (BMRs) and physical activity levels (PALs).' *European Journal of Clinical Nutrition*, 1996: 50 (Suppl 1):S11–23

44. Lieber C. 'Perspective: do alcohol calories count?' *American Journal of Clinicial Nutrition*, 1991: 54:49–55

45. Katzel L.I. and others. 'Effects of weight loss vs aerobic exercise training on risk factors for coronary disease in healthy, obese, middle-aged and older men.' *Journal of the American Medical Association*, 1995: 274(24):1915

46. Egger G., Bolton A. and Cameron-Smith D. 'Prescribing exercise for fat loss in the obese.' *Sport Health* (in press)

47. Despres J-P. 'Physical activity and adipose tissue.' In Bouchard C, Shephard R.J. and Stephens T. (eds) *Physical Activity, Fitness and Health: International Proceedings and Consensus Statement*, Champaigne, Ill., Human Kinetics, 1994

48. Jakicic J.M., Wing R.R., Butler B.A. and Robertson R.J. 'Prescribing exercise in multiple short bouts versus one continuous bout: effects on adherence, cardiorespiratory fitness, and weight loss in overweight women.' *International Journal of Obesity*, 1995: 19:893–901

49. Blix G.G. and Blix A.G. 'The role of exercise in weight loss.' *Behavioral Medicine*, 1995: 21:31–9

50. Egger G. 'Prescribing exercise.' *Modern Medicine*, 1991: 34(7):106–17

51. See reference 50

52. Dolgener F.A., Kolkhorst F.W. and Whitsett D.A. 'Long slow distance training in novice marathoners.' *Research Quarterly for Exercise and Sport*, 1994: 65(4):339–46

53. Egger G. *The Art of Sensible Exercise*. Sydney, David Ell Press, 1988

54. Egger G. and Champion N. *The Fitness Leader's Handbook*. Sydney, Kangaroo Press, 1992

55. Pavlou K.N., Kry S. and Steffee W.P. 'Exercise as an adjunct to weight loss and maintenance in moderately obese subjects.' *American Journal of Clinical Nutrition*, 1989: 49:1115–23.

56. Jakicic J.M. and others. 'Prescription of exercise intensity for the obese patient: the relationship between heart rate, VO 2 and perceived exertion.' *International Journal of Obesity*, 1995: 19:382–7

57. Donnelly J.E. and others. 'Muscle hypertrophy with large-scale weight loss and resistance training.' *American Journal of Clinical Nutrition*, 1993: 58:561–5

58. Jeukendrup A.E. and others. 'Effect of endogenous carbohydrate availability on oral medium-chain triglyceride oxidation during prolonged exercise.' *Journal of Applied Physiology*, 1996: 80(3):949–54

59. Egger G. and Swinburn B. *The Fat Loss Leader's Handbook*. Sydney, Allen & Unwin, 1996

60. Shephard R. 'Fat metabolism, exercise, and the cold.' *Canadian Journal of Sports Sciences*, 1992: 17(2):83–90

61. Montoyne H.J., Kemper H.C.G., Saris W.H.M. and Washburn R.A. *Measuring physical activity and energy expenditure*. Champaigne, Ill., Human Kinetics, 1996

62. Foster G.D. and others. 'The energy costs of walking

before and after significant weight loss.' *Medicine and Science in Sports and Exercise*, 1995: 27(6):888–94

63. Wilmore J. and Costill D. *Physiology of Sport and Exercise*. Champaigne, Ill., Human Kinetics, 1994

64. Egger G. *The Sport Drug*. Allen & Unwin, Sydney, 1984; Bouchard C., Shephard R.J. and Stephens T. (eds). *Physical Activity, Fitness and Health: International Proceedings and Consensus Statement*. Champaigne, Ill., Human Kinetics, 1994

65. Wolfe R.W., Klein S., Carraro F. and Weber J-M. 'Role of triglyceride–fatty acid cycle in controlling fat metabolism in humans during and after exercise.' *American Journal of Physiology*, 1990: 258:E382–9

66. Schneiter P. and others. 'Effect of physical exercise on glycogen turnover and net substrate utilisation according to the nutritional state.' *American Journal of Physiology*, 1995: 269:E1031–6

67. Garrow J.S. 'Exercise in the treatment of obesity—a marginal contribution.' *International Journal of Obesity*, 1995: 19 (Suppl 4):S126–9

68. Garrow J.S. and Summerbell C.D. 'Meta-analysis: effect of exercise, with or without dieting, on the body composition of overweight subjects.' *European Journal of Clinical Nutrition*, 1995: 49:1–10

69. Andrews J.F. 'Exercise for slimming.' *Proceedings of the Nutrition Society*, 1991: 50:459–71

70. Grilo C.M., Brownell K.D. and Stunkard A.J. 'The metabolic and psychological importance of exercise in weight control.' In Stunkard A.J. and Wadden T.A. (eds), *Obesity: Theory and Therapy*. (2nd ed.), New York, Raven Press, 1993

71. Schneiter P. and others. 'Effect of physical exercise on glycogen turnover and net substrate utilisation according to the nutritional state.' *American Journal of Physiology*, 1995: 269:E1031–6

72. See reference 24

73. See reference 24
74. Katch F.I., Clarkson P.M., Kroll W. and Wilcox A. 'Effects of sit up exercise training on adipose cell size and adiposity.' *Research Quarterly for Exercise and Sport*, 1984: 55(3):242–7
75. Wilmore J. and Costill D. *Sports Physiology*, Champaigne, Ill., Human Kinetics, 1996
76. Grilo C.M. 'Physical activity and obesity.' *Biomedicine and Pharmacotherapy*, 1994: 48:127–36
77. Epstein L. and others. 'Effects of decreasing sedentary behaviour and increasing activity on weight change in obese children.' *Health Psychology*, 1995: 14(2):109–15
78. Rauramaa R. and Leon A.S. 'Physical activity and risk of cardiovascular disease in middle-aged individuals.' *Sports Medicine*, 1996: 22(2):65–9
79. Wadden T. 'Obesity prevention following the treatment of obesity: Behavioural and psychological factors.' Paper presented to the 7th International Conference on Obesity, Toronto, Canada, 1994
80. Raben A. and others. 'Evidence for an abnormal postprandial response to a high fat meal in women predisposed to obesity.' *American Journal of Physiology*, 1994: 267:E549–59
81. Hunt P. and Hillsdon M. *Changing eating and exercise behaviour*. London, Blackwell Science, 1996
82. Weisner R.L., Wilson L.J. and Lee J. 'Medically safe rates of weight loss for the treatment of obesity: a guideline based on risk of gallstone formation.' *American Medical Journal*, 1995: 98(2):115–17
83. Egger G. and Stanton R. *GutBuster II: The high energy guide*. Sydney, Allen & Unwin, 1995
84. Prentice A.M., Goldberg G.R., Jebb S.A., Black A.E. and Muratroyd P.R. 'Adaptations to Slimming.' *Proceedings of the Nutrition Society*, 1991: 50:441–58
85. Egger G. and Swinburn B. *The Fat Loss Handbook: A Guide for Professionals*. Sydney, Allen & Unwin, 1996

86. See reference 85
87. See reference 85; Robison J.I. and others. 'Redefining success in obesity intervention: The new paradigm.' *Journal of the American Dietetic Association*, 1995: 95(4):422–3.
88. Burns D. *Feeling Good: The New Mood Therapy*, New York, Penguin, 1992
89. Garrow J. 'Penalties of shifting weight.' *British Journal of Medicine*, 1995: 311:1653–4
90. Jeffries R. 'The truth about weight cycling.' Paper presented to the Australian Society for the Study of Obesity (ASSO) Annual Meeting, Brisbane, October 1994
91. Lean M.E.J., Han T.S. and Morrison C.E. 'Waist circumference as a measure for indicating need for weight management.' *British Medical Journal*, 1995: 311:158–61
92. Hannan W.J., Wrate R.M., Cowen S.J. and Freeman C.P. 'Body mass index as an estimate of body fat.' *International Journal of Eating Disorders*, 1995: 18(1):91–7
93. Tremblay A. and others. 'Alcohol and a high-fat diet: a combination favoring overfeeding.' *American Journal of Clinical Nutrition*, 1995: 62:639–44
94. See reference 24
95. Lieber C. 'Perspective: do alcohol calories count?' *American Journal of Clinicial Nutrition*, 1991: 54:49–55
96. See reference 85
97. Klausen B., Toubro S. and Astrup A. 'Effect of age and gender on 24-hour energy expenditure measured in respiratory chambers.' *International Journal of Obesity*, 1995: 19(2):84
98. Montoyne H.J. and others. *Measuring physical activity and energy expenditure*. Champaigne Ill., Human Kinetics, 1996
99. Prentice A. and others. 'Physiological responses to slimming.' *Proceedings of the Nutrition Society*, 1991: 50:441–58
100. Levitan R.D., Kaplan A.S. and Rockert W. 'Characterisation of the seasonal bulimic patient.' *International Journal of Eating Disorders*, 1996: 19(2):187–92.

101. Formiguera X. 'Health professional approach to weight control.' In Cottrell R. (ed.), *Weight Control: The current perspective*. London, Chapman and Hall, 1995

102. 'Food label claims: what do they mean?' *Choice Magazine*, February 1995; *Code of practice on nutrient claims in food labels and in advertisements*, National Food Authority, Canberra, 1995

103. Corti, B. Unpublished doctoral thesis. University of Western Australia, School of Community Health, 1997.

104. Cardwell G. *Diet Addiction*. Wellness Australia, PO Box 519, Subiaco WA 6914

105. Dietz W. 'The origins and consequences of childhood obesity.' Paper presented to the Australian Society for the Study of Obesity, 3rd Annual Meeting, Melbourne, September, 1995

106. Egger G. and Swinburn B. 'An ecological paradigm for understanding the obesity pandemic.' *National Health and Medical Council Report on the Prevention of Obesity*, Canberra, AGPS, 1996

107. See reference 85

108. Hodges A.M. 'Modernity and obesity in coastal and highland Papua New Guinea.' *International Journal of Obesity*, 1995: 19:154–61

109. Stanton R. *The Diet Dilemma*. Sydney, Allen & Unwin, 1989

110. Brownell K. and Wadden T. 'Behavior therapy for obesity: Modern approaches and better results.' In Brownell K. and Foreyt J.P. (eds), *Handbook of Eating Disorders*. New York, Basic Books, 1986

111. Drewnowski A. 'Intense sweeteners and the control of appetite.' *Nutrition Reviews*, 1995: 53(1):1–7

112. Prentice A. and Jebb S. 'Obesity in the UK: sloth or gluttony?' *British Journal of Medicine*, 1995: 311: 437–9

113. De Graaf P. and others. 'Energy compensation during long-term consumption of reduced fat foods.' *International Journal of Obesity*, 1995: 19(2):27; Gatenby

S.J. and others. 'Nutritional implications of reduced-fat food use by free-living consumers.' *Appetite*, 1995: 25:241–52

114. James W.P.T. 'A public health approach to the problem of obesity.' *International Journal of Obesity*, 1995: 19 (Suppl 3):S37–45

115. Zeni A.I., Hoffman M.D. and Clifford P.S. 'Energy expenditure with indoor exercise machines.' *Journal of the American Medical Association*, 1996: 275(18):1424–7

116. Grilo C.M., Brownell K.D. and Stunkard A.J. 'The metabolic and psychological importance of exercise in weight control.' In Stunkard A.J. and Wadden T.A. (eds), *Obesity: Theory and Therapy*, 2nd ed, New York, Raven Press, 1993

117. World Health Organisation. 'Physical status: The use and interpretation of anthropometry.' *WHO Technical Report Series*, 1995

118. Bouchard C. and Shephard R.J. 'Physical activity, fitness and health; The model and key concepts.' In Bouchard C., Shephard R.J. and Stephens T. (eds), *Physical Activity, Fitness and Health*. Champaigne, Ill., Human Kinetics, 1994

119. Poehlman E.T., Toth M.J. and Fonong T. 'Exercise, substrate utilization and energy requirements in the elderly.' *International Journal of Obesity*, 1995: 19 (Suppl 4):S93–6

120. Blundell J. 'Food intake and appetite control: from energy intake to dietary patterns.' *International Journal of Obesity*, 1995: 19(2):1001–2

121. Malina R.M. 'Regional body composition: Age, sex and ethnic variation.' In Roche A.F., Heymsfield S.B. and Lohman T.G. *Human Body Composition*. Champaigne, Ill., Human Kinetics, 1996

122. Li M. and Bjorntorp P. 'Effects of testosterone on triglyceride uptake and mobilisation in different

adipose tissue in male rats in vivo.' *Obesity Research*, 1995: 3(2):113–19

123. Gleim G.W. 'Exercise is not an effective weight loss modality in women.' *Journal of the American College of Nutrition*, 1993: 12(4):363–7; Keim N.L. and others. 'Moderate diet restriction alters substrate and hormone response to exercise.' *Medicine and Science in Sports and Exercise*, 194:26(5):599–604

124. Rossner S. and Ohlin A. 'Pregnancy as a risk factor for obesity: lessons from the Stockholm and weight development study.' *Obesity Research*, 1995: 3:276S–8S

125. Arroyo P. and others. 'Parity and the prevalence of overweight. *International Journal of Obstetrics and Gynacology*, 1995: 48(3):269–72

126. Hammer R.L., Babcock G. and Fisher A.G. 'Low-fat diet and exercise in obese, lactating women.' *Breastfeeding Review*, 1996: 4(1):29–34

127. Reubinoff B.E. and others. 'Effects of low-dose oestrogen oral contraceptives on weight, body composition, and fat distribution in young women.' *Fertility and Sterility*, 1995: 63(3):516–21

128. Haffner S.M., Katz M.S. and Dunn J.F. 'Increased upper body and overall adiposity is associated with decreased sex hormone binding globulin in postmenopausal women.' *International Journal of Obesity*, 1991: 15:471–8

129. Heiss C.J. and others. 'Associations of body fat distribution, circulating sex hormones and bone density in postmenopausal women.' *Journal of Clinical Endocrinology and Metabolism*, 1996: 80(5):1591–6

130. Treuth M.S. and others. 'Energy expenditure and substrate utilisation in older women after strength training: 24-hour calorimeter results.' *Journal of Applied Physiology*, 1995: 78(6):2140–6

131. King N.A., Snell L., Smith R.D. and Blundell J.E.

'Effects of exercise and macronutrient availability on appetite: is there a difference between males and females?' *International Journal of Obesity*, 19 (Suppl 2): 91(abstract)

132. Hauner H. 'Adipocytes as a source and target of hormones: recent developments in adipose tissue.' *International Monitors in Eating Patterns and Weight Control*, 1996: 5(1):2–5

133. Zhang Y. and others. 'Positional cloning of the mouse obese gene and its human analogue. *Nature*, 1995: 11294:372–5; Shetty P.S. and others. 'Energy requirements of adults: An update on basal metabolic rates (BMRs) and physical activity levels (PALs)'. *European Journal of Clinical Nutrition*, 1996: 50 (Suppl 1):S11–23

134. See reference 24

135. See reference 85

136. Formiguera, X. 'Health professional approach to weight control.' In Cottrell R. (ed.), *Weight Control: the current perspective*, London, Chapman and Hall, 1995

137. Rossner S. 'Realistic expectations of obesity treatment.' In Cottrell R. op. cit.

138. See reference 24

139. Tupling H. *A Weight off Your Mind*. Sydney, Bantam, 1989

140. Lightman S.W. and others. 'Discrepancy between self-reported and actual caloric intake and exercise in obese subjects.' *New England Journal of Medicine*, 1992: 327(27):1893–8

141. Stuart R. *Act Thin, Stay Thin*. New York, 1985

142. Seligman M. *Learned Optimism*. Sydney, Random House, 1992

143. Burns D.D. *Feeling Good: the New Mood Therapy*. New York, Penguin, 1992

144. Ellis A. *How to stubbornly refuse to make yourself miserable about anything, yes anything*. Melbourne, Sun Books, 1988

145. Wysoker E. 'Women's experiences losing weight and

gaining the lost weight back.' *International Journal of Obesity*, 1994: 18(Suppl 2):80

146. Pudel V. 'Psychological aspects of obesity.' In Cottrell R. (ed), *Weight Control: the current perspective*. London, Chapman and Hall, 1995

147. Wilmore J.H. and Costill D.L. *Physiology of Sport and Exercise*. Champaigne, Ill., Human Kinetics, 1994

148. Velthuis-te Wierik E.J.M., Westerterp K.R. and van den Berg H. 'Impact of a moderately energy restricted diet on energy metabolism and body composition in non-obese men.' *International Journal of Obesity*, 1995: 19:318–24

149. Shide D.J. and Rolls B.J. 'Information about the fat content of preloads influences energy intake in healthy women.' *Journal of the American Dietetic Association*, 1995: 95(9):993–8

150. Green S.M. and Blundell J. 'Comparison of the perceived fillingness and actual intake of snack foods.' *International Journal of Obesity*, 1995: 19(2):28

151. Swan G.E. and Carmelli D. 'Characteristics associated with excessive weight gain after smoking cessation in men.' *American Journal of Public Health*, 1995: 85(1):73–7

152. Brundin T., Thorne A. and Wahren J. 'Heat leakage across the abdominal wall and meal induced thermogenesis in normal weight and obese subjects.' *Metabolism*, 1992: 41(1):49–55

153. Richman R.M. and others. 'Weight loss intentions and obesity management.' Paper presented to the Australian Society for the Study of Obesity, Annual Conference, Sydney, 1996

154. Fisher M. *Understanding the 20th century fat cell*. Network Update Seminars, Sydney, 1996

155. Foreyt J. 'Behavioural management of weight control.' National Heart Foundation Symposium: Wrestling with Obesity, Sydney, 1996

INDEX OF TIPS

193

Exercise

Maintaining your losses

The influence of the environment

Behavioural influences

Weight-loss products and programs: the good, the bad and the ugly

The Good